"There is nothing more luxurious
than space to breathe."

– Thomas Pheasant

THOMAS PHEASANT

SIMPLY SERENE

Principal Interior Photography
Durston Saylor

Inspirational Photography
Thomas Pheasant

RIZZOLI
NEW YORK

New York Paris London Milan

Foreword by

Victoria Sant
President of the National Gallery of Art

Contribution by

Jeff Turrentine
An Editor's Reflection

Introduction

Victoria Sant

President of the National Gallery of Art

In this book, you will see plenty of beautiful photos depicting finished Thomas Pheasant interiors and read plenty of thoughtful sentences describing just how he went about finishing them. But I can tell you from personal experience that the marriage of those images and words is still not quite capable of conveying what it's like to see Tom in one of these spaces *before* he sets about turning it into something magnificent.

Someone unfamiliar with how Tom works could be forgiven for wondering, as they watched him silently and solitarily explore a new space, *What is he doing?* Here, I would suggest to you, is what he is doing: he is contemplating the space's myriad possibilities, calculating its potential to provide serenity and comfort, the twin pillars of his style. He is, in effect, seeing the future. If you are fortunate enough to observe Tom at the beginning of a project, as I have been, it is a remarkable thing indeed to witness the intensity he brings to the task of understanding everything there is to understand about a building, a room, a floor — well before he starts to transform it.

Those who know Tom personally know that he is, fundamentally, a generous and kind individual. His elegance and equanimity are integral to his work; they work together in him to create a heightened sensitivity that can almost seem like empathy. I believe that this unique quality is what allows Tom to make a place feel like it truly *ought* to feel, to look as it *ought* to look, and to be, ultimately, what it *ought* to be. His convictions are rooted in an absolute reverence for the building itself; that's where it all begins. And from this starting point of architectural connection, his designs proceed to develop organically, with the final result being so sure-footed that to sit in a Thomas Pheasant room is to sit in a room you simply cannot imagine being any other way. His energy, determination, and fierce devotion to detail inevitably produce, in the end, the most natural and honest representation of a space that there could ever be.

My husband and I have been fortunate to work with Tom on two projects from start to finish: our house in Washington, D.C.'s historic Georgetown neighborhood and our apartment in Midtown Manhattan. On many levels, the two homes couldn't be more different. But what they have in common is the abundant evidence throughout of Tom's unmatched skill in making homes serene, beautiful, and livable — whatever their context. In both cases, Tom's approach was exactly the same. He walked around. He looked carefully. He stood for a while in one place and then in another. As we observed him, we could almost sense him absorbing the entirety of these spaces, not only their pasts but also their futures.

And then, once the spell was broken, he talked to us. He wanted to know what *we* thought, what *we* loved. He wanted to know what we hoped for and, in a very real sense, who we thought we would "be" whenever we were in these spaces. Would we be entertaining? Decompressing? Escaping? Cocooning? Each bit of new perspective we were able to give him expanded his views and informed his designs. As those designs began to take shape — in his head at first and then later on paper, with layouts and elevations — all the glorious details began emerging: the profile of a ceiling, the heft of a door hinge, the edge of a corner. Flooring and furniture and wall finishes and draperies were added next, every one of them selected to reinforce a powerful central idea. Again, and throughout the entire process, he talked (and listened!) to us, factoring our views and reactions into his larger equation.

Tom's work on our two homes utterly transformed their appearances while honoring their respective characters and locations. If I had to identify his ethos — what drives him and separates him, ultimately, from other designers — I would be quick to identify it as this reverence, this respect. Tom has a deep mind and a big heart but a light hand.

In a chapter of the book you're holding in your hands, Tom relates the story of his childhood epiphany under the rotunda in the National Gallery of Art in Washington, D.C. As the president of the National Gallery for the past ten years, I have walked through that space often. Ever since I heard the story of how it served as Tom's earliest inspiration, it seems even more majestic to me knowing, as I do, that it had such a profound impact on a man whose talents I consider truly remarkable, whose dedication I find rigorously complete, and whose personality I find unerringly genial. His appreciation for life and all of its revealed beauty is unmistakable and infectious. Tom Pheasant is, simply, a delight to be around, and his spaces are — equally simply — a delight to live in.

Jeff Turrentine

The word *classical* is bandied about so casually these days in design-magazine articles that it's easy to forget the word actually *means* something. As an editor who's been responsible for seeing many of these articles into print over the years, I've grown accustomed to writers who, in sore need of yet one more synonym for good taste, cite this or that designer's "classical elegance" or "classical approach." The term has become a (rather lazy) shorthand way to suggest someone's personal penchant for understatement or to denote a distaste for chintz.

Meanwhile, a handful of designers like Thomas Pheasant are embodying classicism, *true* classicism, as they set about creating spaces that superimpose modern notions of comfort and luxury over ancient ideals that have proven their worth time and time again, from Ancient Greece to the Roman Empire to Renaissance Italy to Georgian England to Beaux-Arts America. For Thomas, classicism isn't merely an effect — or merely an affect, for that matter. Instead, it's a set of sacred principles that guides him like a compass, steadfast and ever true, as he navigates the mysterious terrain of a new residential project: a place where the map of a client's desires doesn't always match up perfectly with the map of a designer's instincts, and where any number of exigencies can throw an uncertain traveler off course.

I first encountered Thomas' work in two dimensions, as pixelated images on a computer screen in my office at *Architectural Digest* magazine, where I served as both a senior editor and contributing writer for the better part of a decade. Witnessing his designs, even under those decidedly less-than-optimal circumstances, was a revelation. Here was a designer whose rooms and furnishings were simultaneously bold yet familiar-seeming, sleek yet comfortable, ethereal yet rooted. At first I couldn't quite figure out how he — of all the different designers whose work I engaged with regularly — had managed to reconcile

modernity and tradition so successfully, making this highly-difficult-to-pull-off merger look so effortless, so *natural.*

And then, once I actually walked through a Thomas Pheasant–designed residence for the first time, it dawned on me. The words I scribbled down in my notebook that day — descriptors like *thoughtful, ordered, edited, tailored, balanced, complete* — also happen to be the stylistic building blocks of classical architecture, which takes as its starting point the idea that design is not only capable of affecting our moods and spirits, but is also indeed *obligated* to usher us from one state of being to a new and more exalted one. By granting physical form to eternal principles of serenity and equipoise, so the neoclassical theory goes, our inhabited spaces can carry us toward solace, contemplation, and self-betterment.

If we think of classicism as a style that emphasizes the principles of order over chaos, harmony over tension, quietude over stridency, and balance over imbalance, then I would wager that Thomas Pheasant is the purest exponent of classicism working in interior design anywhere in the world today. These first principles are also his first principles; it's impossible to imagine him ever volunteering to stray from them, and I sometimes wonder if he would even be physically capable of doing so should some perverse spirit try to force him. But curiously, he's not a neoclassicist in the conventional sense of that term. Search his designs for evidence of a pediment or a Corinthian column or any other stalwart emblem of antiquity, and you'll end up searching in vain. Thomas traffics in ideas, not icons; he distills the essence of classicism and incorporates it into wholly original, highly modern work.

Not all interior design is art — not by a long shot. But design, when it's done at its highest level, is indeed art — and it's art that is in the unusual position of being forced to make the case for its own value anew every single day,

because it's art that we actually *live* in. Anyone who has observed his process knows that Thomas approaches his designs the way an artist does, and during that process he aspires to answer the very same questions that art has long been tasked with answering (or at least attempting to). On a technical level, what specific combinations of light and dark, line and curve, presence and absence, can be achieved to affect our sensory appreciation of a creative work? And on a markedly more spiritual level, what, fundamentally, *moves* us, inspires us, makes us feel valued and productive as humans, happy to be alive?

What *does* move us? Civilization will stipulate certain obvious examples: the painted image of raucously colorful flowers in a Giverny garden, a moonlight sonata, a lover's sonnet. But what about a room, a beautifully proportioned, light-filled room, appointed with objects and furnishings so perfectly crafted or chosen that they seem to be not simply *in* it but an integral *part* of it, every bit as essential to it as its walls or ceiling? A room that encourages us, through the careful attention that has clearly been paid to even the smallest and finest of details, to reexamine the small, fine details of our own lives? A room so natural and comfortable that it almost seems to breathe, and in doing so invites *us* to breathe?

Vitruvius wondered; Palladio wondered; Frank Lloyd Wright and Jean-Michel Frank and Syrie Maugham wondered. Thomas Pheasant wonders, too. He answers, happily, in the affirmative, and that answer is to be found in these extraordinary rooms, where classical philosophy and contemporary style sit in a matching pair of Thomas' white tufted Athens lounge chairs: two learned friends discussing the history of the Greek *klismos* from antiquity through the machine age. Classicism and modernism aren't natural antagonists, as it turns out. They have plenty of ideas to share, plenty of interesting things to say to one other. They just need more people like Thomas Pheasant to bring them together.

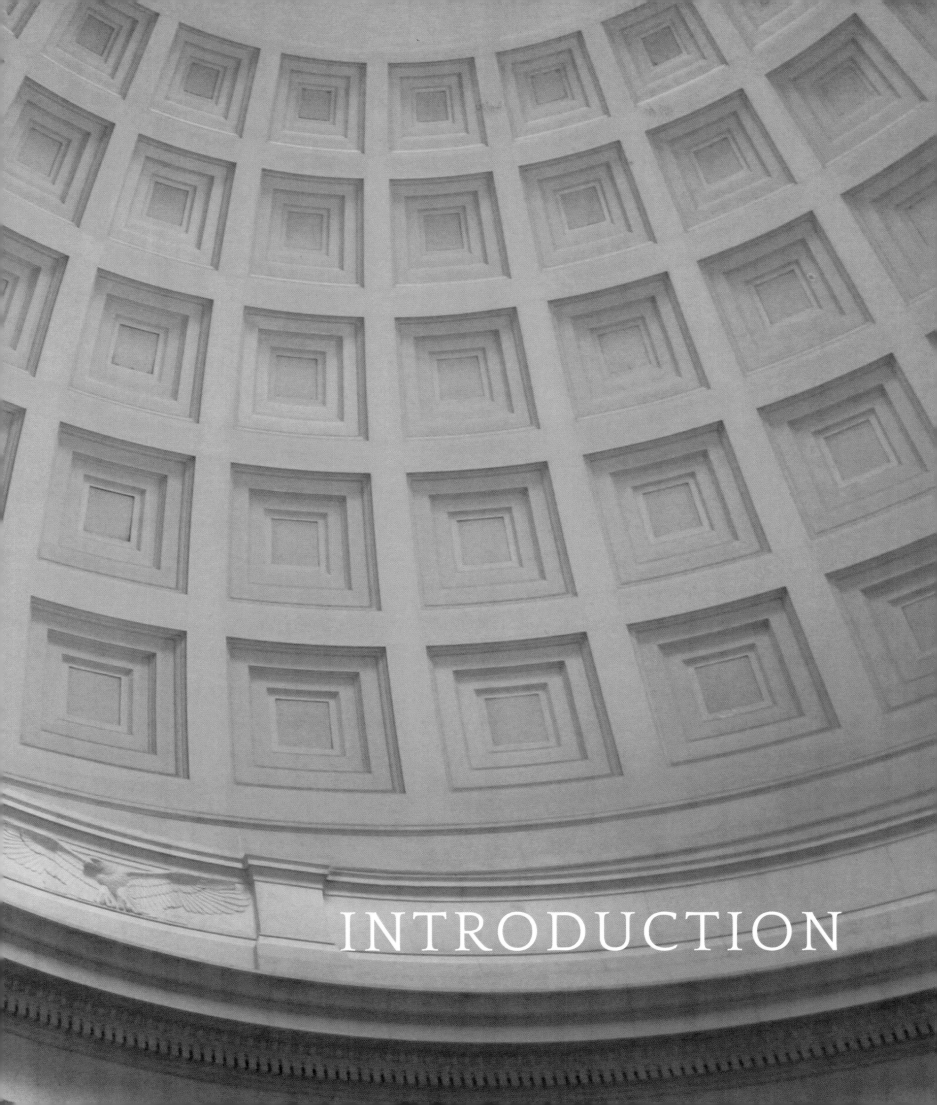

INTRODUCTION

Ten years ago,

a publisher approached me expressing an interest in putting together a book about my interiors. Naturally, I was excited at the prospect of seeing my designs captured in the pages of a beautiful oversize volume on the shelves of my local bookstore, alongside those about others whose ideas and projects I've long admired. And so I began thinking seriously about how best to present my work in this way. I created a rough outline, organized primarily by general ideas that seemed like they might naturally correspond to book chapters. I was off to a promising start, I thought.

It was, however, truly only a start. Months went by, and between obligations to clients and a demanding travel schedule, my work on the book was constantly being interrupted. Busy months turned into busy years. But I never did give up on the book, and whenever I could I would return to my outline, picking up where I had left off – revisiting ideas, rethinking chapters, reviewing images. And I often told myself, You know, it's probably just as well that I've waited this long, since I want to be sure that

this project (i.e., whatever project I happened to be working on at the time) makes it into the final mix.

Now, of course, I realize that the central paradox of creating a book about one's designs is that the designs themselves are organic, fluid, and evolving, whereas a book – while it can be beautiful and even inspirational – is a static and unchanging document. And so I came to the conclusion that even more satisfying to me than a book showcasing my individual designs would be a book about my individual design *philosophy:* not just a collection of pretty pictures, in other words, but a book that used images and words to illustrate the fundamental principles that are at the heart of my work.

As I imagined this volume over the past decade, all of my various working titles for it inevitably contained within them the word *classical.* Now that word, *classical,* is clearly one that I'm comfortable with, and anyone who knows my work at all surely knows that the legacy of classical architecture has been a

major influence on it. But as the last ten years have rolled by, so too have a stream of design books that reference, in one way or another, classical style: *Modern Classical, The New Look of Classical Design, Living in Classical Style, Classical Country, Classical Dog Houses.* (okay, I made that last one up. But I bet it's in production, even as I type.)

And so while I don't mind the label, I've ultimately come to believe that perhaps it doesn't really describe my work – the final, realized product – so much as it describes my method or my approach. To put it another way, I know that I'm influenced strongly by classical ideals of harmony, symmetry, order, quietude – all those qualities that come to mind whenever we think of the great works of classical or Renaissance design. But I also know that I personally strive to look forward, not backward. Which is why I was certain, beyond any doubt, what the title of this book needed to be: *Simply Serene.* To me, that's what all of those timeless classical ideals are working toward: serenity, a sense of absolute comfort, and absolute peace.

I still remember, vividly, the first time that all of those classical design elements came together to create in me that feeling of serenity. Back when I was in the third grade, my classmates and I boarded a bus in our suburb of Adelphi, Maryland, and rode into Washington, D.C. to visit the National Gallery of Art. As we filed into the building, we were directed to stand together in the grand Italianate rotunda – quietly, without fidgeting – and await the arrival of our tour guide. As I did so, I stared up at the top of the coffered dome and then around me at the slender, volute-topped columns of black marble. Sun poured down through the rotunda's oculus and bathed the space in a faint blue light. The noise from my chattering classmates faded away, and I momentarily forgot that I was part of a larger group. I suddenly became aware of a feeling I was experiencing, a feeling that took me quite by surprise. It was a complicated sensation, but it could be boiled down, paradoxically, in just five clear words: *I want to live here.*

Later, I would learn all about the rotunda's architect, John Russell Pope, a man who designed not only the National Gallery of Art but also the Jefferson Memorial and the American Museum of Natural History in New York. Pope was a rather lonely figure,

hewing almost religiously to his neoclassical aesthetic at a time when his architectural peers were just beginning to experiment with all of the ideas and techniques that people had taken to calling modernism. A certain bland and institutional variant of modernism would, in fact, eventually become the style of architecture associated with so many structures in Washington, D.C. – those countless beige (or more often gray) office buildings that emerged in the decades after World War II and still serve, perhaps fittingly, to house large and largely faceless federal bureaucracies.

Pope must have anticipated that these buildings would gain currency and come to dominate the city's low-slung skyline. He felt strongly, however, that the fundamental principles of his beloved neoclassicism – order, harmony, symmetry – more properly celebrated the great achievements of mankind that a national art gallery was designed to showcase. Art is timeless, thought Pope; so too, then, should be any building that is dedicated to art. Neoclassicism represented to him a direct and unbroken architectural line that began with the ancients of Western civilization and went right up to the present, linking us all. It was a style that was, at its core, profoundly humanist.

I didn't know any of this, of course, in the third grade. All I knew was that I liked to draw animals and people, mainly, or perhaps occasionally a castle. I hadn't yet made the connection between my casual draftsmanship and any notion of design. But my experience that day at the National Gallery became a part of me, a part that was content to stay inside me quietly until such time as I was ready to make more sense of it and turn it into something else. It ended up becoming the single most important event of my youth, and possibly my life.

The words that mysteriously echoed in my head that morning – *I want to live here* – eventually became the basis for my entire career. Before I even knew what the word serenity meant, I had experienced it, viscerally and profoundly. As soon as I began my design career, I dedicated myself to creating spaces that, once completed, would compel me, my clients, and anyone who happened to be visiting to utter the same phrase.

And now, with this book ten years in the making, I hope to share with you the elements that inspire that same utterance.

ELEMENTS

9

It's safe to say

that no two designers — even two who might share a similar aesthetic and cite the same major influences — would ever go about creating the same interior. Simply put, the process is too personal. A client could use the same highly specific language to tell a dozen different designers precisely what she wanted, and she would nevertheless get a dozen different results. Each one of them might very well be spectacular in its own way. It's the last part of this statement, the "in its own way" part, that makes my chosen field so dynamic and fun. Every project affords a new opportunity for growth and expression. How many people get to say that about their jobs?

One of the most wonderful things about my job is that it's not *just* my job. It's my life. The mental and creative processes that I use when I'm conceiving and building a new space are the same ones that guide me through the rest of my world. Somewhere along my career path, these processes have come to define how I visualize reality. It goes far beyond how I approach the various challenges related to space or color or furnishings. These processes constitute my road map, my creative filter, my way of connecting to practically everything around me.

I compare it to learning a new language. In the beginning, there's a period defined largely by the enormous conscious effort that's required to recall vocabulary and translate words and sentences in real time. Later, however, comes the hardworking student's reward: the moment when fluency is achieved, when the new language becomes spontaneous and natural. In both the fluent and pre-fluent states, the speaker may be capable of speaking clearly and of understanding and being understood. But only one of those states allows the speaker to be completely relaxed while communicating — and to take full advantage of the confidence that comes from that relaxation.

For me, fluency in the language of design means having the confidence to take chances and push boundaries, while at the same time feeling absolutely secure that my own work is rooted in something solid and timeless. Though each project necessarily comes out differently, I rely on the same principles and conceptual tools every time — in just the same way that the speaker of a language must rely on the same inviolable rules of grammar and syntax to come up with different sentences that reflect different thoughts and ideas. My goal in writing this book is to share these principles

and tools so that my work can be experienced by readers not simply as pictures on a page but as articulated steps in a well-defined process. I didn't want to write a how-to book, not by any means. I wanted to write a "How come?" book, one that would explain precisely why I think this particular process, based on these particular rules, works as well as it does.

In these pages, I have attempted to articulate this process and the underlying rules that define it. Whether I am discussing the crucial importance of defining a home's architecture early on, referencing classical ideals in laying out a floor plan, finding ways to inject color into a neutral palette, editing the final details, or engaged in any other part of the long and involved act of designing a space, I'm hoping to convey how distinctly important each of these individual steps is to the realization of the whole. Take any one of them away and the process falls apart entirely. But perform each of them with the utmost care and the result is a coherent, harmonious, beautiful creation.

"Over time, and with lots of practice,
the process became far more intuitive."

This process doesn't take place in a vacuum, of course. The larger context of the client's wishes informs every decision that's made along the way. For me, that tightrope walk — balancing what's best for the space and what's best for the client — isn't a source of frustration but one of creative energy. A designer must, above all, be conscious of the fact that he or she is hired to create homes for other people, many if not most of them strangers who are trying to put together a "dream home," an opportunity that may come around only once in a lifetime. When I take on a new project, then, I am essentially being asked to serve as a guide for clients as they embark on a lengthy, not to mention expensive, journey. Though we may have met only recently and agreed to work together based on a few hours of conversation, they are placing in me a tremendous amount of faith, trusting that I'll be able to make real what they have only imagined.

Here is where being a good listener comes in very, very handy. In the throes of that early courtship between myself and a new client, I have to be able to intuit not only *how* they live currently, but also how they *want* to live: how, in other words, their new home or renovated space will help them fulfill the basic human desire to grow, to change, to evolve. Sometimes I'm given just a few hours to spend alone in a space before an agreement is reached; during that time, I have to juggle the tasks of defining the space's architecture, laying out the rudiments of a floor plan, imagining the style and scale of furnishings, conceiving a palette, and — maybe most importantly, at this stage — discovering the secret connection between the clients and the space they've chosen, how it reflects their unique spirit and sensibility.

Years ago, at the beginning of my career, this system of planning and procuring was, quite frankly, labored and overdetermined. My decisions tended to be motivated much more by the fear of making a mistake than by the sheer pleasure that comes with that wonderful blend of immersion and intuition. But over time, and with lots of practice, the process became far more intuitive, and the fear of making a mistake was replaced by confidence and the joy of new ideas and new opportunities. I was, you might say, becoming fluent.

Though my internal thought processes have evolved dramatically, one thing that hasn't changed over the years is that I require a good chunk of time within a new space spent in quiet, and even solitary, observation. Many new clients must wonder to themselves as they watch me disappear into my own thoughts, "*What is this guy thinking about?*" As a matter of fact, I'm fairly certain this question arises in the minds of my staff as they wait (patiently!) for me to share my thoughts. But the simple truth is that this time — the time I spend alone, inside my head, connecting with the space — is the time that I enjoy the most during the entire design process.

When I'm in the midst of it, I feel like I'm collecting the clues that will help me solve a grand mystery. Sometimes an important clue announces itself in a flash of revelation; at other times, it teases and taunts and resists immediate discovery. But always it's exciting and energizing — and, to put it plainly, fun. Linguists say that you know you're fluent in a new language when you start speaking it in your dreams. To me, walking through an empty space and imagining it living up to its full potential is a kind of waking dream. And nothing feels better, as I glide through this dreamscape, than feeling like I understand what the space is trying to tell me.

ARCHITECTURE

As a child

growing up in suburban Maryland, I became obsessed with old Hollywood films. And for me, none could match those that starred Fred Astaire. These fabulous black-and-white movies, often set within dreamlike interiors that presented classical architecture in a grand but ethereal style, offered me a kind of celluloid glimpse into design heaven.

I choose that word *heaven* quite consciously. The effect of these films on my young psyche was not unlike what some designers and architects say they experience upon first entering the great cathedrals of Europe, whose original architects were attempting to relay a human vision of what God's house must look like. While I watched Fred and Ginger waltz effortlessly up and down alabaster steps or glide across an elegant loggia, I felt like I was seeing a place where all things were perfect and where everything and everyone resided in harmony. It was, like my epiphany beneath the National Gallery's rotunda, an early realization that interiors can evoke highly emotional responses.

The young boy watching these films from the rec room of his parents' split-level was utterly transported. Then, a few years later, I came across the great movie *Auntie Mame*, starring Rosalind Russell. This film introduced me to the idea that someone could actually change the decoration of their space and create, from what already existed, a totally new one. The revelation inspired me to renovate my own bedroom almost immediately thereafter, elevating it from child eclectic to modern. I sawed off the legs of my triple dresser, dyed my beige chenille bedspread black, and exposed my unfinished wood floors by removing my blue shag wall-to-wall carpet. The renovation resulted in a slightly unlevel chest of drawers, a mouse-gray bedspread, and the presence of exposed carpet-tack strips around the perimeter of my room. But how exciting – how thrilling! – to know that I could control my environment.

The lesson I learned that day was that the very first step in any kind of renovation is to look around and take careful stock of what's already there. Creating a serene interior begins well before the selection of furnishings, colors, and collections. One begins, essentially, by defining the architectural vocabulary of the space.

If you're lucky enough to be carrying out your design program within a home that's both beautifully detailed and thoughtfully planned, then you are fortunate indeed. Because the sad reality is that most spaces simply aren't architecturally fulfilling – and in those all too rare instances where they are, they often don't meet the practical requirements of daily life, spatially speaking.

Over the past thirty years, I've accompanied countless clients as they walked through countless spaces in the hopes of purchasing their dream home. These spaces have ranged from historic houses with beautiful architectural features – but built decades before the advent of cook's kitchens, walk-in dressing rooms, or even master bathrooms – to new condominiums that offer all the modern amenities and jaw-dropping city views but can boast all the architectural charm of a shoe box.

I'm not even going to mention the sprawling builder-conceived developments that have spread like kudzu vines through our suburban neighborhoods. They, along with the aforementioned, make up the bulk of choices that people have when they begin choosing their next home. Turning any one of these into a beautiful, serene space is a challenge, to put it mildly. Still, it can be done. I know it can, because I and my team have done it, over and over again. It takes imagination, careful planning, and a lot of trust. But it really is possible.

"My interiors do not begin with furnishings and decoration...
there has to be a strong architectural foundation on which to build."

Most of the images used in this book are taken from projects where I acted as both the interior designer and the interior architect. In these projects, my duties as the latter necessarily preceded my duties as the former. I know from the very outset of any project I take on that my interiors are going to be dependent on the architecture, and that's why I take so much time initially studying it, thinking of ways to refine it and enhance it. Before we've bought even the first stick of furniture for the clients, my team and I have already done all that we can to understand and strengthen the architectural vocabulary. It simply must be this way: our interiors cannot rely on furnishings and decoration. There has to be a strong architectural foundation on which to build.

Mapping that foundation can actually take a little time, and occasionally I'll have clients whose eagerness to paint and upholster and furnish has made them impatient with that part of the process during which my team and I are walking around the residence, nodding our heads silently, snapping photos, and taking notes. But the truth is that this quiet, reflective, seemingly low-energy work is absolutely crucial. It's sort of like traveling to a place where they speak the same language you do but in a slightly different dialect: You can't hope to accomplish anything until you've made sure that you truly get what's being said. You have to study the local vocabulary — including all the intonations and connotations and references — before you can communicate effectively. Interior design, when it's done properly, is in conversation with architecture; the goal is always to make that conversation sensible, meaningful, and uplifting.

I've also enjoyed the rich collaborative experience of working with great architects. In these instances, the results can be truly amazing. The architect suggests things that might not have occurred to me; I suggest things that might not have occurred to the architect; and the clients are right there to guide us and shape our thinking as we go along.

But whether you've assembled a dream team of architects and designers to create your home from scratch or are beginning your project within the confines of an existing one, the first step — always — is to establish the architectural vocabulary and develop the flow accordingly. In all of my interiors, I place ultimate importance on detailing every single space, from the first step of the entry to the most remote corner. My methods aren't necessarily simple, but my methodology is: I approach every room as if it were being created to stand on its own, without the benefit of any kind of decorating camouflage or the introduction of paint, fabric, or dramatic furnishings to fulfill it.

The larger point I want to convey is this: a truly beautiful room is beautiful long before it's ever decorated. The most important job that I or any designer can do for a client is to discern what's already good about their home's preexisting architecture and coax out its best details, refining them and emphasizing them. Or if those details simply aren't there, to invent new ones in a manner that's harmonious, pleasing, and logical.

Then we can begin the process of decorating — ideally with a light hand — and creating whole interiors that leave room not just for my clients' objects and furnishings but also for their ever-evolving lives. I take great pains to make my rooms feel clean and comfortable, so that the architecture can reveal itself and there's room to grow. I consider it to be a failure of interior design when homes are decorated so densely that people have nowhere to go and nothing to add. When every wall and table is covered — when there's no room to bring in a new concept or installation, or even just to honor a fond memory by putting up a picture or a keepsake — the designer has gone too far.

Making a strong design statement doesn't have to mean filling an entire room full with furniture and heavy draperies. The statement can — and should — include flexibility, the capacity for a space to evolve as the client makes new discoveries and wants to incorporate them. My style necessarily acknowledges and respects not only the choices that were made in the past by the architect, but also those choices that will be made, at some point in the future, by the client. The overall vision is balanced, fluid, and flexible. *Serene*.

"Once defined, the architectural vocabulary should flow throughout the house linking each room to a clear vision."

CLASSICAL PRINCIPLES

Why do some rooms

just feel *right*, whereas others decidedly do not? Or maybe it's better to launch this discussion with a different but related question. Why is it that when you're walking through the streets of, say, Florence, you so often find yourself compelled to stop in front of a beautiful centuries-old portico and appreciate it for a moment? For many people, this need to pause and marvel — and that's really what it feels like when it strikes you: a *need* — isn't easily explained; it operates on the visceral level of inescapable urge. I believe it reflects a fundamental human sensitivity to a very specific category of beautiful design: a sensitivity that allows us, in the here and now, to connect directly and almost mystically to a creative thread that has coursed through centuries.

Our understanding of the world around us is determined, to a very large extent, by our sense of vision. That sense of vision, in turn, places images into categories of harmonious or inharmonious, lovely or unlovely, based on how well those images match up to certain models of perfection that we hold, consciously or unconsciously, in our minds at all times. And those models have endured for so long because they express certain principles that were identified thousands of years ago and have come to be known since then as the building blocks of classicism. *They* are the reason that some rooms just feel right. For those who aren't involved day to day in the task of design, it's not essential to grasp the underlying mechanics of these principles

and how they interrelate in order to enjoy the feelings they elicit. But for those of us who are involved in such tasks, a full comprehension of how these principles work together is absolutely key.

Balance, proportion, and unity are among the fundamental classical compositional elements that should be evident in every aspect of a designer's work. From floor plans and elevations to furnishings and finishing touches, they are required if the goal is to create something that can be said to be serene or harmonious. But while I know from my own education that such principles are capable of being taught and understood, I also believe that no amount of academic training can match the knowledge to be gained by actually spending time inside the beautiful spaces that adhere to these principles, time spent observing them in detail and soaking up their quiet majesty.

For my part, whatever confidence I may have in my ability to transmit these ideas in my own work comes from the essential combination of my formal study *and* my informal immersion in great rooms from the past and present. Information is certainly found in the former. But revelation is found in the latter.

And revelation requires patience. It doesn't come from glancing quickly over your shoulder and snapping a photo as you walk past one of the world's great facades. To truly connect, you must *experience*.

I'll never forget the time I invited my parents to visit Paris in order to share with them my deep love for French culture and for a city that has been so influential for me. I had arranged to take them to Versailles one day during their trip, although I was slightly concerned that my father might find the tour overlong and uninteresting. Though he had always been proud of my work, in truth he wasn't very interested in things like museums or designs that he couldn't boast as being his son's.

As we made our way through the tour, I suddenly noticed that my dad wasn't there. My first thought was that he had quickly passed us and was waiting outside by the car. Nevertheless I decided to backtrack, moving through the maze of rooms in reverse order to see if I could find him. And in fact I did find him, standing by himself in one of the more beautiful rooms in this most amazing collection of beautiful rooms, just staring, happily lost in the moment and in his thoughts. I stood quietly watching him look. I recognized the expression of contentment on his face; it had been the expression on my face too, as I had almost certainly stood in that exact same spot and experienced the same feeling that he was experiencing now. Even with no formal understanding of design, even with no real interest to speak of in this amazing palace or its rooms, my father had connected with beauty on a deep and profound level. I wanted him to have that moment and, later, for him to be able to remember it.

33

"Symmetry and balance are amazing tools in striking that peaceful harmony within a room."

I find it amazing that given how many beautiful examples there are in this world of what works, examples that are literally just sitting there and waiting to be studied, we are nevertheless still plagued by so many iterations of bad design. What's even worse is that so many of these bad designs are classically inspired. I worry that they are becoming so common that we may be slowly numbing ourselves into a passive acceptance. Our newer suburbs are filled with high-end housing developments yielding row after row of houses marked by a distorted, Disneyfied vision of classicism. There are entire subdivisions where the presence of a columned breezeway or a pediment over the front door is supposed to tie the architecture, somehow, to something ancient and noble. It's a sad state of affairs we find ourselves in, but at the same time it should also be noted — with equal amazement — that even with all the examples of poor design lining our streets, people are still able to recognize true expressions of pure classical theory when they encounter them.

At the top of the list of principles is clarity. Oftentimes as I walk through houses or apartments with clients who want me to help them develop their interiors, I am confronted by an overcomplicated floor plan: a sure sign that the residence has been subject to an insensitive renovation that has yielded, among other unfortunate results, a confusing progression from room to room. You can't merely decorate around a bad plan. Until that plan — the foundation, after all, atop which you'll be building your interiors — is thoughtfully reorganized, no attempt at redesign or renovation will ever be successful. Look at the floor plans of Palladio, or of any of the indisputably great architectural wonders; in them you'll instantly detect a perfect, easy-to-grasp organizational clarity.

No less essential than clarity to the establishment of serene, harmonious spaces are the related qualities of balance and symmetry. I have learned over time that human beings respond deeply to these qualities, even when they don't perceive them on a fully conscious level, such as when they have been subtly incorporated into a floor plan or furnishings plan. Balance and symmetry, whether they're obvious or not, send the brain a subliminal message that all is well, all is organized, all is being taken care of, and that highly comforting message allows us to *relax*. Conversely, if a space is imbalanced or contains objects whose different scales pit them against one another proportionally, we sense conflict or chaos. And, understandably, we get anxious.

"It is my personal connection to what
I have seen and what I have experienced
that has sharpened my focus and directed
my vision of how spaces should be."

The simple act of loading bookshelves with books or objects can offer insight
into the psychological virtues of balance. As anyone who has ever attempted
it knows well, it can be hard to turn a wall's worth of shelves filled with books
and other unrelated things into anything approaching a harmonious, unified
assembly. Here is where the counterintuitively named notion of asymmetrical
balance — wherein elements are distributed unevenly but in such a way that
their masses and proportions strike the eye as being roughly equal — can
sometimes prove much more effective than the conventional "one on the
right and one on the left" approach that people tend to take. Visual balance
isn't about matching things; it's about controlling emphasis and establishing
equilibrium. When it has been achieved, even on a bookshelf, we may not
wind up with perfect symmetry. But we will be able to sense the balance,
and that's what produces the calm within us.

Lastly, I'm a firm believer in the importance of unity, the ability of all elements
in a design to cohere and create a sense of oneness. As I've already
mentioned in other chapters, I typically begin any project by defining the
space in purely architectural terms — long before I turn my attention to things
like paint, fabric, or furnishings. As I progress from an architectural focus
to furnishings, I am always thinking of the whole. It is a process of bringing
together finishes, details, and furnishings in a combination that makes each
piece relatable to and dependent on each other.

Whether I'm working within a staunchly traditional vocabulary that calls
for added restraint or a more contemporary one that frees me up to
explore new ideas or techniques, I know that by trusting and reaffirming
my connection to these classical principles, I'll end up with a space that's
beautiful, balanced, and coherent. And it won't just be evident to *me*. It will
be evident to everybody who sets foot in it, even if they're not really giving it
much thought. The room will simply feel...*right*.

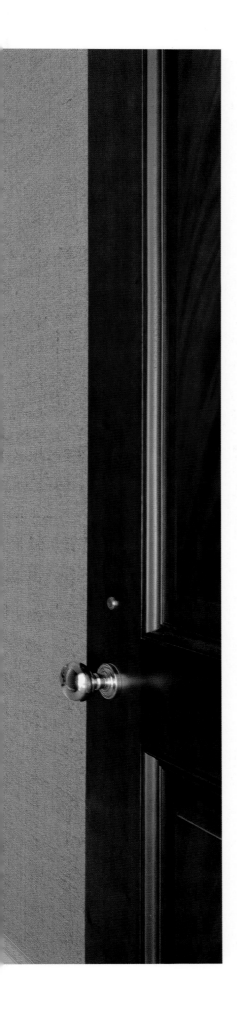

Fabric wall coverings bring immediate depth and interest to any room. Whether you upholster walls in simple woven silk or rich velvet damask, the effect is instant warmth. *Above,* the scale of the room determined the proportions of the mantel and door casing and even the selection of the gilt frame. The deep-toned wall fabric works perfectly to reinforce tradition while bringing sharp contrast and focus to the crisp white mantel and trim. *At left,* the placement of this French clock in front of the convex mirror commands your attention and is a conscious play of circles. It is this subtle relationship between objects that I find most interesting. The nubby raw silk wall covering was introduced to relax the elegant formality of the room's furnishings and symmetry.

NEUTRALS

The first home

I ever designed for myself was a turn-of-the-century townhouse in Washington, D.C. Somehow, despite the fact that the house was utterly uninhabitable and I was just out of college and had very little money to my name, I managed to convince a bank to allow me to take out a mortgage. I ended up gutting the entire place and creating a modern and really quite simple interior whose architectural energy derived from one very special feature: a centrally located spiral staircase, gorgeously illuminated by an enormous skylight, which linked each level of the house. I painted everything white and covered the floors in a dark gray industrial carpet. By the time I had completed my renovation, I was somewhat discouraged to learn that there was no money left for me to buy any furniture. No matter: I threw some gray leather pillows around, and that was that.

The local newspaper ran a story on the house in its home section. The photos were beautiful, and I can remember the feeling of excitement that washed over me the day the article came out: I was being presented to my fellow Washingtonians as a new, young, "radically spare" interior designer. I stayed close to the telephone in anticipation of all the calls that were about to start pouring in from potential clients. Somehow it hadn't occurred to me, in the throes of my excitement, that late-1970s Washington, D.C., might not be the perfect time and place — from a purely commercial perspective — to be spreading a gospel of tranquil minimalism. While I waited for the phone to ring, I had plenty of time to look around my new house and marvel at its simply conceived beauty. Whether my neighbors were ready for this look or not, I already knew just how fulfilling it could be to watch something as simple as the sunlight moving through this space and to witness the interplay of light and shadow as they danced together across the volume of my central stair, switching leads depending on the time of day.

Later I would come to realize that I had essentially built for myself a fully inhabitable, multistory black-and-white photograph — by which I mean that my lifelong love for black-and-white photography and my love for creating (and living in) what might be called neutral spaces are inextricably linked. In both, what I value the most is the absolute freedom that's granted to the eye: the freedom to roam calmly and slowly along surfaces, to find beauty in tonal contrasts that range from the very sharp to the extraordinarily delicate. I love the way that shapes and forms reveal themselves in both, not via explosive shocks of color but via subtle gradation that requires time and concentration to discern. This is how I like to look at photography, and this is how I like to enjoy space.

In a way, I've really adopted this as my primary design goal: the simple presentation of a fluid spatial experience, one that requires some time before its depth can be appreciated fully. Color is an important part of this process, to be sure. But the experience can't be constructed by selecting and overfetishizing a single color, or even a few of them. It's a slow and deliberate process that combines forethought, instinct, and very careful editing.

I can lose myself for what feels like hours inside a beautiful black-and-white photograph. Similarly, I've found that there is something just as magically calming and contemplative about a room that has been enveloped in the shades borrowed from a single chromatic palette. But this is where caution must be urged: for those who would paint or upholster their interiors in the endless variations of white, gray, or beige to be found these days, it will soon become clear that these wonderful neutral shades all by themselves aren't able to confer that much-sought-after tranquility. I can't count how many times friends or acquaintances have complained to me that they did everything so tastefully *right* — "We painted our walls white! We covered our upholstery in expensive bone-colored linen!" — only to find that their interiors, in the end, fell hopelessly flat.

What they were missing, almost invariably, were the contrasting elements that define that light palette in the first place: think of the black (or more likely, the gray) in a black-and-white photograph. A restricted palette absolutely requires the artful layering of elements — well-defined silhouettes, an interesting assortment of textures and high-relief surfaces — if it is ever to move beyond being just a plain, light-colored room and become a truly beautiful and fulfilling one. Every one of these individual elements contributes to the whole in a crucial way.

"Neutral palettes place focus on the form and quality of every element within a space."

For starters, if you've committed to the idea of a neutral-toned space, then there's already a good chance you're the type of person who believes that visual distraction is the enemy of beauty. And if that's the case, then you've presumably already taken a close look at the architecture of the room — its fundamentals — to make sure that things like the proportions of its windows, the size and placement of its doors, and the character of its moldings aren't going to be pulling your attention away from what you want to be seeing and sensing when you walk into it. (I've said many times that for a space to be truly beautiful, it has to be considered beautiful even when devoid of any furnishings. That's why I invest as much time as I do obsessing over walls, floors, and architectural details.)

Think of the neutral-toned room as a space that hides nothing and reveals everything. It's a little like putting a white leotard on an imperfect body: those imperfections will instantly become magnified and very, very distracting. If you're going to paint your walls and trim in a single neutral color, then you'd better make sure that the surfaces of those walls and the profiles of that trim have the strength and integrity to carry the burden of all the attention that will inevitably be coming their way. If you're not asking the eye to think about color, the eye — on its own — will decide to think about form instead.

It should go without saying that the same rule holds true for any furnishings upholstered in neutrals. The silhouette of that particular chair or sofa is going to become the visual focus by default, so choose these pieces with the utmost care. When selecting them, I always suggest trying to view them in muslin or plain fabric first before committing to them finally. Review each piece for its sculptural quality, and be absolutely ruthless in your critical evaluation. Look for beautiful lines and immaculate workmanship; accept nothing less. Then invest in the very best upholstery you can afford when the time comes to cover them.

Rooms filled with exciting and bold-patterned prints can be wonderful, but there's no denying that they allow the visual impact of the fabrics to dominate at the expense of everything else. In neutral spaces, by comparison, fabrics play a supporting role and allow the eye to travel around the room, soaking up all the other details you might prefer to showcase: the unique and sensuous curve of an exquisitely crafted settee, the architectural statement made by your moldings and finishes, the personal statement made by an especially well-edited collection. The thing to remember, of course, is that the flip side of these neutral spaces' unending generosity is their unforgiving nature when the interior architecture is poor or the details unremarkable. Don't let that be the case.

Form is key in a neutral room, but so is layering. Juxtaposing the shades from a single palette so that different tones and textures are allowed to play off of one another is what gives a neutral space a sense of depth and complexity. The same understanding of contrast that a genius like Henri Cartier-Bresson used to turn photographs into high art can be employed to turn a living room or bedroom into a sanctuary. Contrast can come in the form of well-placed accents, or it can come in the form of a bold background that draws worthy objects in the foreground into high relief. Picture a metal window frame. *Now* picture it with a unique bronze finish. Picture a pair of mahogany interior doors. *Now* picture them set against starkly, brilliantly white trim. Picture the folds of a simple neutral drapery fabric. *Now* picture that drapery hanging by means of visually graphic, one-of-a-kind metallic hardware.

Just as it does in the greatest photography, the energy from a neutral-toned space comes less from the form or tone of any one object and more from the formal and tonal *relationships* between adjacent objects. Go to a museum or gallery, or pick up a well-designed art book, and spend some time looking at beautiful black-and-white photos. Take the time to linger over the images, to savor their complexity, and to discover how the seemingly opposed notions of contrast and harmony are actually connected to one another — bound together holistically like yin and yang. It will give you tremendous insight into how to go about building an interior using variations on a single tone.

Neutral spaces give you wonderful opportunities to bring focus to the architectural details of your home. I have found that opening these spaces to natural light helps magnify these details through the gentle play of light and shade. This same light helps to capture the sculptural silhouettes of carefully selected furnishings.

CONTRAST & TEXTURE

Linking a room's

surfaces and objects together through the tonal varieties to be found within a single color is one way to build a serene interior, and it's obviously one that I believe in strongly. But a monochromatic room can't work if it doesn't contain some sort of kinetic counterpoint. Once the neutral palette has been established, supportive elements must be added in order to confer dimension and depth. These supportive elements are contrast and texture.

I'm on record as a staunch champion of classical principles such as harmony and unity. But there's a time and a place for tension and friction too. If you want to spotlight something or draw attention to it somehow, you have to distinguish it from something else. Contrast and texture are how you go about doing it. The key is to use these elements with reserve and purposefulness.

The basic idea is to punctuate points of interest in a plane of vision by directing the eye through a space just as a melody carries you through a song. Mishandled, contrast leads to confusion and chaos; you can easily eliminate whatever focus you're hoping to strengthen by scattering too many contrasting elements throughout a room.

Some designers like to declare their love for a particular object, fabric, color, or whatever by declaring that "you can never have too much" of it, whatever it is. Trust me, you can have too much of *anything*, and in design, as in all other parts of life, too much of anything can just simply be too much. I understand that there are designers out there who yearn to cover every inch of their interiors in black-and-white zebra-print fabric, but for me, that's camouflage decorating that attempts to unite a space by forcing it to bow to a single idea.

The neutral-toned room can suffer a similar fate if it doesn't allow contrasting forces to intervene. When they're present, those contrasting forces serve to ground the design and heighten the intensity. For a quick lesson in how it all works, one need only spend a little time studying the art of the greatest black-and-white photographers. Figures such as Edward Weston, Man Ray, Irving Penn, and others showed us that when light and shadow are locked in a tight embrace, drama and intrigue are born. Cinematographers and set designers for old Hollywood black-and-white films were aware of the same thing: even without the benefit of color, they knew that entire realistic worlds could be suggested

simply by knowing how and when, precisely, to juxtapose light and darkness. By thinking along similar lines, I find that I am able to use these same principles of visual contrast to direct the eye from one object to another and one space to another, almost as if it's being choreographed.

Throughout this book, I have purposefully depicted many of my interiors using black-and-white, as opposed to color, photographs in order to make certain points about form. Art instructors often use black-and-white images when they're trying to teach their students about the primacy of form. Once color has been (literally) taken out of the picture, the eye of the student has little choice but to focus on things like shape, scale, and volume. When we look at black-and-white images, our brain is forced to use its power to interpret what it sees differently. It must rely on the subtle differences between light and shade to interpret what is being presented. From a designer's standpoint, anything that makes somebody look at something longer and more carefully is a plus. Why not use these same principles to steer the eye in a particular direction and then have it linger there for a while?

"Contrast ignites the choreography of
directing the eye from one object to another...
in essence, it tells the eye where to go."

Being the more tactile of the two supportive elements, texture can allow us to move through one color while providing a vast array of interesting surfaces. It is contrast but not in the context of light and dark. It is the use of smooth against rough, leather against wicker, silk against tweed that creates distinction. It can be used to bring focus to an object as well as inform us on mood or formality. It is an essential tool in any design plan that calls for layering: combining textures on a single plane of vision is an instant way to suggest richness and depth, even when all of the textures are drawn from the same palette.

Contrast and texture are absolutely crucial to my own designs. Just as the lighter portions of a black-and-white photo are what help define whatever darker image is being captured, so too do these supportive elements help define the look and feel I'm after in each room by stopping the eye for a moment, slowing it down, giving it a linear path to follow. They are vivid examples of a fundamental truth about good design: it's never about an item or an object or a theme. It's about the relationship between all the different things that you see and how they work together seamlessly — sometimes by carrying an idea forward and sometimes by interrupting an idea ever so slightly, just long enough to make you think about the idea for a second before moving on.

One of the first pieces of furniture I created was the *Lens Ottoman* shown **above.** It is a perfect example of my interest in bridging the past and present. This classical form was made modern through simplicity of form and its bold black lacquer finish. Within the context of this traditional Georgian library, it was used to infuse an unexpected modern element. To relax the traditional mood of the room, I introduced the natural textures of light linen upholstery and sisal carpeting. **At right,** the dark mahogany niche was designed not only to showcase this stone art deco torso, but also to bring dimension to a room filled with pale neutral tones. The graceful frame of my *Athens Lounge Chair* is fully realized within this sea of neutrals.

"Through the use of light and dark, I am able to create interior windows that allow me to layer my spaces. This is something I have learned from studying great black-and-white photography."

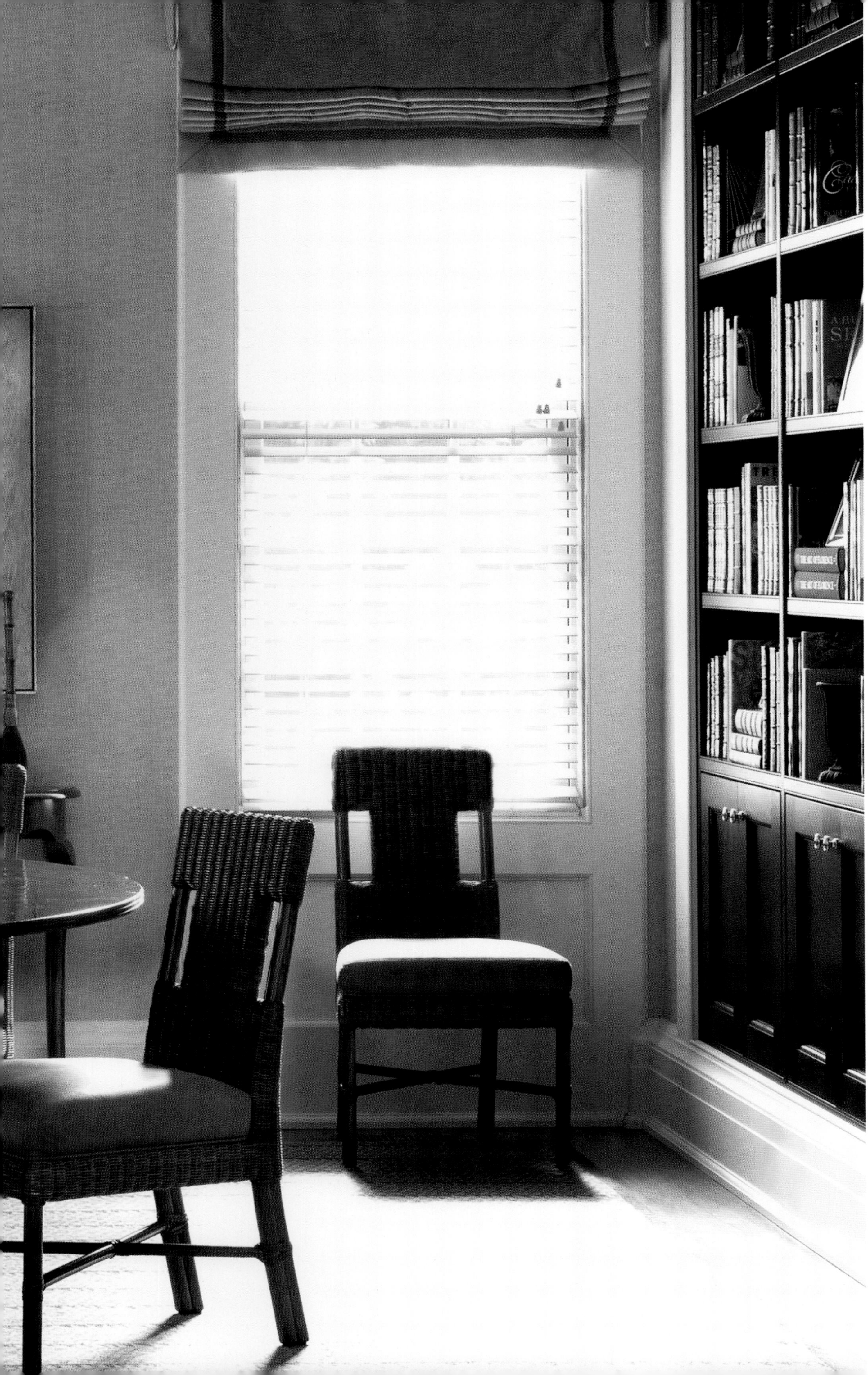

COLOR

A few years ago,

I was approached by someone who had recently attended a party at the home of one of my clients. In a tone of voice that suggested he might actually want to work with me, he exclaimed that he loved everything about the house...but that the project's neutral tones just weren't for him.

It's never been any real secret that I'm particularly fond of the so-called neutral palette. Look at an example of my work from any design magazine and you'll very quickly grasp that I have a special affinity for the boundless iterations of snow, limestone, and slate. So when this potential client-to-be made his pronouncement, I was more than a little surprised.

I asked him his favorite colors. He responded, without hesitation, "Red and orange."

Without any hesitation, I quickly responded, "*Together?*"

"Whenever possible," he replied matter-of-factly.

Quickly I tried to shift the conversation to other topics that might put us on some kind of common ground: modern vs. traditional styles, tile vs. stone, carpets vs. hardwoods, the proper size and placement of television sets. But as we talked, my mind kept wandering back to his honest, unabashed admission. Could I ever really hope to give this man the home he dreamed of, and — assuming that I even could — wouldn't I end up having to compromise my most closely held beliefs about what constitutes a serene room in order to do so?

But then I noticed something else about him. As he went on to describe what, exactly, he so loved about my client's home, he was actually saying all the right things. He had noticed the layout of the rooms, the symmetry of the entry hall, the details I had incorporated into the millwork and ceilings. He had admired the style of the furnishings, the manner in which I had mixed the Tibetan rugs and the upholstered walls. And then, just as I was torturing myself trying to decide if I was really and truly the right designer for him, he said it.

"But of all the things I love about that house, what I love most about it is the tranquility."

With this one phrase, he had me. Convinced that his ultimate priority and mine were one and the same, I simply couldn't pass up the challenge to do what I love to do most within a very different chromatic context than the ones I was used to working in. Then and there I knew that I could, and would, find some way to turn his preferred color palette into a neutralized background that could serve as an elegant showcase for all of the different elements I try to incorporate into my interiors.

Because I knew that he understood the essence of what I try so hard to do — make tranquil spaces — I couldn't let the issue of color become a wedge between us. We agreed to work together, and it turned out, no surprise, to be one of the most exciting and satisfying collaborations I've ever had. (For the record, I did manage to convince him to segregate the orange to one space and the red to another.)

I share this story not only because it's a great example of how clients have played a huge role in challenging me to reach beyond my comfort zone as I hone my signature style. It is, in fact, a great example of that, but it's also something more. It's a wonderful illustration of what color is and what it *isn't* in a design. Color is something that can be played with, employed strategically, intensified, made more subtle, brought to the foreground, moved to the background, and a million other things. But color isn't *ever* a set of aesthetic handcuffs. In fact, it's just the opposite.

Color can easily be neutralized when incorporated into both furnishings and surroundings. This combination always leads to an easy and open atmosphere. *At left,* the soft blush-colored chair upholstery works with the natural tones of the sycamore table and wall details to create a warm overall glow for this New York dining room. *Above,* a client's love for the peaceful tones of sky and water led to my selection of this unified palette.

"Color can be one of the ways my clients can express themselves...my job is to provide them the perfect canvas."

I approached this client's project exactly as if he had asked me to give him a home done up in a hundred shades of ivory. The living room – a living room which, I noted with mild anguish, would have been the *perfect* stage for one of my own personal favorite shades of ivory – was instead clad in numerous permutations of red. In that room and others, russet fabrics in a variety of textures were brought together to cover the lean, well-tailored furnishings. Ebony chair frames and dark wood paneling added extra depth and contrast to all the stark red silhouettes. The direction for the family room's palette was determined upon the selection of a truly fabulous carpet in shades of brilliant orange and saffron. For that room's fabrics, I found yet another iteration of deep red to punctuate the colors found on the floor (colors I had already, by this point, excitedly begun thinking of as my new family of "spicy neutrals") and to tie this room to similar reds that could be found in the rooms leading up to it.

The result was a home bathed in colors that I didn't typically use, and I absolutely loved it, all of it. Just as I had hoped, I was able to translate my general ideas about the role of neutrals from a light palette to a dark, bold one. I had effectively "neutralized" red and orange, so that instead of usurping all of the attention in a room, they were forced to follow the same rules that I ask more conventional neutrals to follow. By layering different shades and textures – from light to dark, from sleek to rustic – I turned them into a context for the house's handsome interior architecture, for the fine furnishings, for the personal items that my client and his family wanted people to experience visually as soon as they walked in the door. The feeling given off by that context was indisputably warm and inviting: it was red, it was orange, and yes, it was tranquil.

Here's the thing to remember: people can be intimidated when choosing color, since they sense it as being the biggest and most irreversible commitment they'll be making to a room's overall look. And they're right – up to a point. But color can actually be expressed in uncountable ways beyond those big, basic commitments we make to upholstery and paint. When you're operating within the confines of conventional neutrals, things like art, flowers, or even the spectacular view onto a garden or cityscape afforded by a picture window can bring bold, dynamic color into a room in precisely the amount, and with precisely the intensity, that you choose. No more, no less.

What's more, taking this strategic approach to adding bold color to a room confers a second, and very important, gift: flexibility. Bright flowers, artworks, and objects can (and should!) be changed and moved around with as much frequency as we desire, in keeping with our ever-changing moods or even just the whimsy born of a particular moment. Rooms need to evolve in order to live. Keeping the essence of a room neutral but interjecting color by means of the small, personalized, and above all variable items within it allows for maximum expressive freedom.

A very dear client once asked me, somewhat apologetically, if I thought it would be okay for her to put artificial flowers in vases, thus relieving herself from the constant burden of refreshing her home weekly with newly cut bouquets. I responded by asking her, "Would you invite a mannequin to a dinner party?" But it wasn't just the artificiality I was objecting to. A display of even the most realistic-looking silk flowers will stay in their vase... *forever*. During that time, they will go from perfectly lovely to unremarked upon to innocuous to invisible. By putting fake flowers in a vase, she would have been robbing herself not only of a lovely opportunity to connect with the natural world, but also of the opportunity to place, and then *replace* real flowers, entirely different ones of entirely different shapes and lengths and smells and colors. By simply introducing a new and colorful bouquet of flowers – these wonderful things that bestow their beauty upon us for such a short time – we're graciously allowed to take part in a meaningful pageant of renewal.

It's amazing how often, while entertaining friends or family in my home, someone will ask me, "Did you do something new? The house looks... *different* somehow." Often all I've done is rotated a piece of furniture from one room to another, or purchased a new artwork, or maybe swayed from my passion for white flowers by introducing an amazing arrangement of purple hydrangea. But whatever it is I've done, I'm aware that I've subtly altered the balance of color in the room, and *this* is what causes my guests to experience the house in a new way, even if they don't quite understand how or why. This, not coincidentally, is exactly the same instant flexibility I want my clients to enjoy in their own homes. And it's as powerful a testimonial as can be made for the magical freedom that neutral spaces grant us. Remember that neutral rooms are not necessarily about the absence of color, they are simply a vehicle to showcase that which you find important or beautiful...even if just for a moment.

Even a bold color can bring forth a sense of calm and ease. *At right and above,* I have implemented strong shades of saffron and orange in the same way I use my neutral palettes of ivory or gray. This family room was engulfed in various textures and shades of one color. The result is a focus on the silhouettes of the objects and furnishings throughout the room and not the sudden accent of a bold color. The selection of any color can be directed by the preferences of the client, but the effect of this serene outcome relies on the commitment to that one color experience.

"Neutral rooms are not necessarily about
the absence of color, they are simply a vehicle
to showcase that which you find important."

SCULPTURE

There is something

very special about the physical relationship we have with three-dimensional objects. Perhaps it is because we are programmed to use our eyes to make constant subconscious judgments relating to space and the objects before us, and too often we rely on that subconscious state to supply only the needed information to get us through the day. Here is where the art of seeing requires a little exercise. Just as in any skill, seeing requires a true conscious effort. And like any skill, you must practice this visual exercise regularly in order to make it a true part of your ability to see and, in seeing well, discover and learn.

A perfect example is captured in the image I selected to lead this chapter. One fall afternoon in Paris, as I exited from a design exhibition held at the Hôtel Marcel Dassault something new caught my eye. I was standing at the front entrance when I looked down and noticed the graceful curve of the stone baluster as it wound its way down along the staircase. I grabbed my camera and took this photo. I had visited this building numerous times over the past ten years, and as many times as I had climbed up and down these stairs, I had never experienced this exact moment of physical and conscious alignment.

I have always appreciated the beauty of this building and the overall impact of its design, but how delightful to have this beautiful element present itself to me in a quiet and unexpected way.

Of course, it is the contribution of each piece of a building or space that creates the whole, but once you have taken in the overall impact, it is the actual study of each part that holds the secrets to its success. When visually isolated and detached from this grand building, the sculptural quality of this stone wall is amazing. The architect, Henri Parent, was able to look within a mass of stone and imagine this lyrical curve. The recognition of this effort is something that requires only the ability to stop and, with a conscious eye, allow yourself to take in what you are seeing.

I firmly believe that the ability to recognize beauty is the first step in the ability to create it. Just as I am firmly committed to the idea that you must physically experience great spaces to connect to the ideals of proportion, it is that same physical understanding that is necessary to help you build a strong foundation in designing spaces or objects within them. How you interpret these experiences is up to you,

but you need to hone your awareness to allow these experiences to take place.

Any space can take on sculptural qualities. Even the careful use of rectangular sheets of drywall can produce amazing effects in defining space and creating movement within a room. It only requires that you look at a space or a room as an object, slowly contemplating it as something that should offer more than empty space needing to be decorated. And just as a piece of furniture can be infused with sculptural grace, so can a room.

Sometimes it is the space that leads to the selection of just the right furnishings or presents me with the opportunity to design a unique piece, but there are also times where the furnishings or collections of a client may guide the design of the space itself. Either way, it is the relationship between the space and the objects within it that we experience. This experience is not a flat presentation but a three-dimensional volume that we enter and move through, experiencing endless points of view. Even the most familiar spaces should have the ability to surprise us with a moment of beauty not yet seen – just as I experienced the curve of Henri Parent's stairway in my photo.

"When observing any object,
it is the form that speaks to me first."

It is also important to think about the dynamics between objects within a room. Forms relate to forms. Even a lamp can take on a special importance when paired with just the right object. Whether clients take the time to study each and every composition of their home or simply *sense* the balance and ease within the placement of objects, the result is the same. It is the conscious or subliminal recognition that the room is in harmony which brings us an internal ease and comfort. It is in this harmony that I believe you can allow the space for the individual beauty of each object to be expressed.

How the sculptural form of a table relates to the graceful form of a sofa is difficult to put into words. For me, it is the realization that if I place the same critical eye on every piece within a room, the chances for success are great. Perhaps there is a common thread amongst all the things I find beautiful that creates this easy dialogue between objects. Certainly it is in the art of presenting that these objects can be given their opportunity to shine.

In my own process of designing interiors and furniture, I implement the same eye of experience when sculpting away at mass to reveal the form. I am certain that it has been through my study and appreciation for sculptural beauty that I have come to enjoy this art of designing. Michelangelo often said that every block of stone has a sculpture inside it and that it is the task of the artist to discover it. Why shouldn't this concept apply to the way we shape our rooms and the objects we design to live within them?

...BUT A THING CREATED IS LOVED BEFORE IT EX

"Sculptural qualities can be infused into the space itself...these qualities are not exclusive to the objects placed within."

"Furniture should offer more than practicality. Every piece should have the ability to engage the eye."

SIMPLICITY

Perhaps the most

difficult element to master, simplicity can be one of the most beautiful aspects of any design. As I have claimed many times, simplicity is not simple. It requires confidence and a sure hand. Ultimately, it is the ability to get to the essential without the distractions of the unimportant. So what does this mean?

First, let me be clear how much I enjoy and respect many designers whose work incorporates the ideas of excess luxury and complicated interiors that are saturated with collections, color, and details. As a matter of fact, through the skill of these opulent designers, I have been both delighted and inspired. And while I profess to the glory of simplicity, I am equally aware of the talent and knowing that is required to produce a room that is, for lack of a better phrase, over the top.

But these rooms aren't all created equal. So what is it that makes one of them a breathtaking marvel and another one just full of lots and *lots* of stuff? I maintain that this difference — between conscious, well-wrought over-the-topness and mere loudness — is actually akin to the difference between *simplicity*, which denotes an extraordinary level of care and deliberation, and *simple*, which in the end denotes little more than the quality of being unadorned, unfreighted, or uncomplicated.

As I continue to evolve as a designer, I find that I am motivated more and more by the idea of creating interiors and furnishings that are able to say more with less. It's not just a process of removing objects and details from a room for the sake of having fewer elements in the final equation. It's about really getting at this aforementioned definition of simplicity, about arriving at the deep inner core of a given space or object, the better to reveal whatever is pure — and thus genuinely fulfilling — about it.

As you explore the images throughout this book, each project presented me with a unique set of objectives and demands. While developing the interiors for a very diverse clientele, I incorporated my love for simplicity, listened to the clients as they expressed their goals, and, at the same time, acknowledged the physical realities surrounding and sometimes limiting each project. It can be a bit of a juggling act, but the results should always yield a home that could only have come together for that particular client in that particular space.

At this point, I should emphasize that simplicity is not the same thing as minimalism. The two notions are often confused, and while minimalism does have its foundation in many of the same ideas of less is more and paring things down to their essential natures, minimalism can have the unfortunate tendency to harden into dogma, whereas simplicity, thankfully, never does. As such, simplicity, unlike minimalism, can't really be thought of as a style on its own; rather, it is an aspect of design development that I find deeply rewarding.

I aim for simplicity in my more traditional interiors just as I do in my more contemporary ones in country homes or Manhattan apartments. In these or in any projects, simplicity forces me to ask myself, What is this space really about, and what *isn't* it really about? The answer to that general question helps me answer the highly specific ones that necessarily follow: What will work in here, and what won't? French or English? Eighteenth century or Twenty-first? In order to fulfill my obligations to my clients, the space, and myself, I have to use simplicity's scalpel to keep cutting away at what's extraneous. Only once I've done that can I feel sure that what remains truly *belongs* — that the elements will be working in concert to help the space reflect its true nature. When simplicity isn't factored into that process, distractions begin to mount, and rooms can quickly lose their focus.

Just because a wall doesn't have something on it or a corner doesn't have something in it doesn't mean that something is necessarily missing. Simplicity rewards the fewer objects it allows by giving them more space, presenting each one as a uniquely beautiful thing to be appreciated not just as part of a set, but also as an individual creation. This worthy goal can only be achieved in an environment free of distraction – although it should go without saying that it can also only be achieved if the thing is really and truly beautiful. A collection of mediocre vases sitting atop an ill-proportioned console may indeed fill up a wall, but the result neither commands (nor deserves) the same attention as a single remarkable object that has been well-placed above an equally remarkable cabinet. Simplicity dictates that the eye will go to that single remarkable object naturally, and once it arrives it will rest there and absorb its beauty for a while.

Simplicity is this basic principle elevated to the level of philosophy. I was reminded of that philosophy's enduring value as I went about the business of selecting the images that appear in the different chapters of this book. Every day, I'd rotate images between the various sections; one day, the photos in the "Contrast" chapter moved to the "Simplicity" chapter before moving yet again to the "Architecture" chapter. As frustrated as I may have been at all of the photo juggling, I had to admit that it only confirmed how consistently dependable simplicity is as my guiding compass. I might also add that this compass merely points me in the right direction. I believe that the true art of simplicity is a lifelong study.

Every piece contributes to the wholeness of a room. Therefore, every piece needs to be beautiful. While this seems to be an obvious idea, I am amazed how often we allow our spaces to become filled with things that are mediocre and detract from those things deserving our focus. *At left,* the stunning torsos in these Mapplethorpe photographs are meant to be the focal point of this view. The simplicity of fabrics and surrounding forms give these photographs the space they deserve. Once these images have been contemplated, there is time to appreciate the sculptural quality of the chairs and the individual beauty of the objects on the desk. *Above,* the simple presentation of a single succulent can be as beautiful as any other surrounding element. The key is to give the eye space to move through the room so that wherever it lands, it finds something beautiful to enjoy.

"Simplicity is not simple...it is the process of fulfilling
an idea using only that which is essential."

"I find reward in giving space to each object and
allowing each piece the ability to present itself."

Creating beauty through simplicity is reliant on building appropriate backgrounds and careful use of restraint. Through successful incorporation of these ideas, one of the greatest joys of simplicity is the ability to celebrate both the humble and the extraordinary. *At left,* a simple bouquet and a well-crafted basket gracefully fulfill these vignettes. *At right,* within this very controlled arrangement, I have combined several beautiful pieces against a very simple background. The importance of these particular objects did not require unnecessary decoration. In fact, I find the restraint in this presentation extremely elegant.

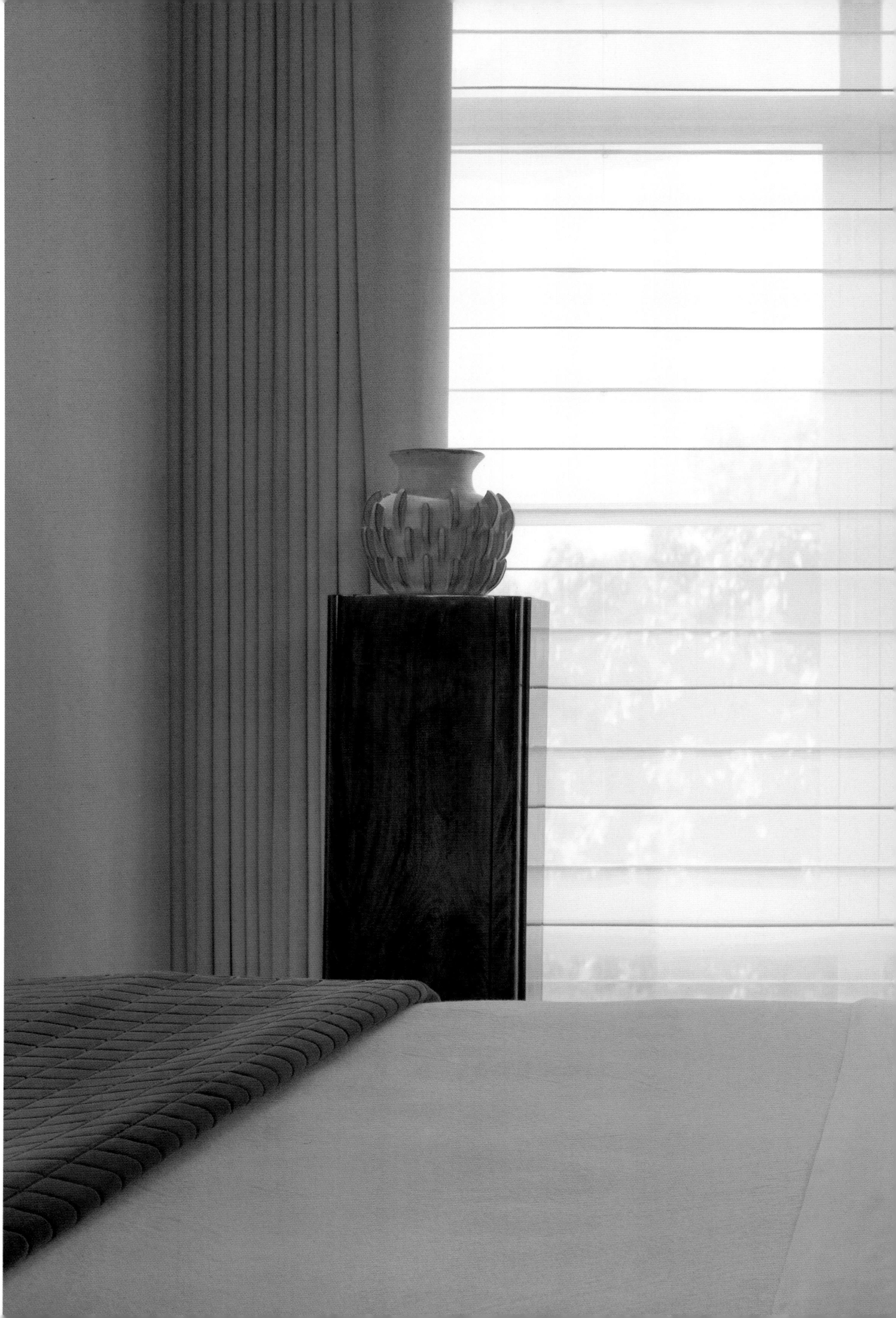

DETAILS

I have always

believed in the immense value of those subtle, slow-to-emerge epiphanies that await the individual who spends the time required to take in, and take in fully, a truly beautiful room.

For some people, the idea of a beautiful yet simple room is hard to grasp. We are all conditioned, in this day and age, to respond to stimuli, stimuli, and more stimuli. But when a room has been well crafted, even the simplest space can reveal stunning depths of creativity. Like a blossom that unfolds at its own natural pace, a room ought to demand that the observer linger for a little while if he or she wants to experience its gifts.

Rooms that derive their energy from things like bold-print fabrics or dynamic wallpaper patterns can be creative too, of course. But to me, the pleasures of such rooms are that much less satisfying for the immediacy with which they announce their notable qualities. These types of decorative devices can provide dramatic impact, but their relentless imposition can be tiring. It is, for me, like turning up the volume on a radio and leaving it on loud...every day.

There's also something slightly tyrannical about a room whose sheer decorative forcefulness refuses to allow for the client's true personality to be reflected in any way or for any new ideas to be introduced after the fact. In rooms like this, what passes for detail is often really just the bravado of a daring sofa or wallpaper pattern. In stark contrast to a room like this one, the serene room demands of its admirer time and – yes – concentration. It generates its very different kind of power via the layering of details and the gradual introduction of objects. It is the opposite of obvious. When you do finally crack the code for discerning its mysteries, the discovery is thrilling: your attention is held that much longer and your appreciation is that much greater due to the fact that you had to focus just a little in order to receive your prize. In a room that emphasizes details over drama, *you* get to control the experience. In a room where the emphasis is reversed, the room controls you.

And there's another difference, too. Serene rooms whose details are revealed slowly more closely mirror the manner in which we live our lives. Joy and delight don't hurtle toward us all at once; they come to us in special moments.

Wisdom and insight don't scream at us; they tend to whisper. I love incorporating into a room the subtle but meaningful architectural or material details that are capable of surprising someone in this way. Even in my most traditional interiors, I always find a way to include details in plaster ceilings or wood paneling or door hardware, all of which make fine places to give the client tiny, unexpected gifts.

I actually spend a great deal of time making these details look like I haven't spent much time on them at all. For a detail to have the magical and surprising quality that I'm after, it has to appear effortless. And by effortless, what I mean is that it should look absolutely, positively at home in its environment. If it does, no matter how surprising or unexpected a detail may be, it will feel right and true; but if it doesn't – if it has clearly just been introduced into a room so that it can stand out – it will create tension. By dominating the conversation between the other elements in the room, it will effectively end up killing that conversation. And to me, the ongoing conversation between these different but intimately connected elements is *everything*.

"The details within a room should
reveal themselves slowly...each being an
unexpected discovery."

I have experienced very creative interiors that introduce brilliantly startling
details or elements that are meant to steal your attention. In most of these cases,
no matter how creative these interiors are, they are of the moment or designed
to provoke a specific reaction. This is not what I aim for in my design. By uniting
a room through materials, scale, and palette, you're investing it with a singular
character. In doing so, you're building a solid and dependable platform: an
emotionally uncomplicated stage that can graciously accommodate change as
well as any number of thoughtful details you might fancy. At the beginning of any
new project, when I'm assessing how every element in a room, from paneling to
railings and floors to ceilings, will work together to express the room's essential
architectural vocabulary, I'm necessarily thinking big. But some part of me is
also thinking small: I know, at some point, I'll want to be adding details of the sort
that will bring a smile to my client's face upon that moment of initial discovery. I
may not have any idea at that point what those details will *be*, but I know I'll want
to be adding them.

On walls or on floors, in furnishings or in fabrics, over the front door or over
the fireplace, details are opportunities for playfulness, poignancy, and pure joy.
They're the subtle twists and inspired ideas that elicit tiny gasps of surprised
delight. They are, without a doubt, what clients love the most about any home
that a designer gives them. They're what make custom furnishings *custom*, and
special attention *special*.

COLLECTIONS

171

Webster defines collection

as, "the act or process of collecting...an accumulation of objects gathered for study or exhibition." It is an active and ongoing process that can be one of the most important elements in the personalization of an interior.

Collecting can also be the one word that helps me rekindle a client's excitement after it has ebbed somewhat during the long and occasionally tedious process of building an interior. Over many months of planning and execution, the constant and seemingly endless parade of decisions to be made can overwhelm some people. Choices about tiles, appliances, finishes, furniture, lighting, bath fixtures, etc., can drain clients of much of the energy that propelled them at the project's outset. It's not uncommon at all for clients to turn to me after a certain point, usually several months into a project, and say with evident exasperation, "Tom, honestly, whatever you decide to do here is fine with us."

While I'm perfectly comfortable making these decisions, there are certain junctures along the way that allow me to pull clients back into the stream of activity where the decisions are not only important but also actually *exciting* for them to make. The point at which we discuss the role their collections will play is one of them.

As a designer who is constantly being exposed to beautiful things, I've had to learn to pace myself when it comes to collecting for my own home. The temptation to acquire pieces

and artworks, to convince myself somehow that I *need* them, is ever present. Thankfully, time and experience have helped me exercise restraint and judgment, even as they have also taught me that surrounding yourself with things that you love can be a source of immense and lasting joy.

A great example: Years ago, an antiques dealer showed me a small bronze box made by the brilliant French designer Line Vautrin (1913–1997). I was already familiar with Vautrin's spectacular mirrors, but not with her boxes. I was immediately taken by this small but exquisite bronze box. My chance discovery soon turned into a focused collection. I now own approximately thirty-five of these charming pieces, and I am always, vigilantly, on the lookout for more. I cannot walk past my collection without smiling. Should a friend or guest ask me a question about my Vautrin boxes, I can actually feel my energy level rise as I go into describing each one. The joy this collection gives me is real and enormous and personal. I want my clients to have that experience too.

As it happens, many of my clients are already in possession of amazing collections when we first meet and begin working together. I've used a number of these collections — of artworks, porcelain, antiques, or even animal skulls — to help me as I went about planning a design, knowing as I did that these things which meant so much to my clients would certainly need to be a major part of that

design. In truth, incorporating my clients' beloved collections only makes my design process that much easier. When they share with me the objects they love above all else, they're granting me direct and immediate insight into their personalities. And since my chief goal is to connect client and interior on an intimate, emotional level, it's a bit like being handed a shortcut-filled road map into how to make the project successful.

Working with clients and their collections, I've gained a new knowledge of and new appreciation for objects that don't necessarily reflect my own personal tastes or interests. This is where I sometimes have to push myself outside of my own comfort range as I explore ways of incorporating these things into my larger design plan.

Recently, a lovely couple that had been collecting contemporary art glass for many years hired me to assist them in their move to a new location. I knew very little about the origins or contents of their collection, and although I had seen similar glass pieces in galleries around the world, this particular art form had never really caught my interest. But during my first visit with them, the clients walked me through their collection piece by piece. They shared with me memories of when they had first discovered the pieces, stories of the relationships they had formed with the galleries where they'd purchased them, and even stories about their relationships with the artists themselves.

"Given that new collections take time,
it is in the planning of the interiors that
I try to build for the future."

I spent a good amount of time with them that day walking through their home and learning all about art glass. Of course, what I was *really* learning about was my clients: their shared passion, which is to say the genuinely romantic connection they have to their collection. In the process, other things became evident: the joy they took in having been married to each other for so many years, the pride they took in their children, the delight that their travels had brought them. They seemed to regard the project we were about to undertake together as an adventure — and their pieces of glass as loved ones who would be coming along with them. All in all, it was a wonderful afternoon, and I returned to my office full of excitement.

What was also exciting, but every bit as challenging, was the fact that the couple would be leaving their gracious, generously scaled residence and moving into an apartment that was half the size. While the new apartment was large, it didn't have the high ceilings and large corridors that naturally allowed for the showcasing of their collection. And so we worked together on editing it down, and I convinced them that together we could find a way to present their very favorite works as a collection within a collection. As the new apartment came together, it was fascinating to see how the process of editing altered the impact of the pieces, both collectively and individually. Some that hadn't stood out so vividly in their former home now seemed bigger and bolder. The clients, rather than expressing sadness that they couldn't share their new space with every last one of their loved ones, were thrilled at how the simple act of recontextualizing certain pieces seemed to give the pieces new life and vibrancy. For me, the whole experience proved to be a fantastic education — not only in the world of art glass but also in the importance of connecting to clients through connecting to the things they hold most dear. And all I had to do to receive this valuable education was listen.

Not all clients are collectors, of course. Sometimes I don't have the luxury of that clearly marked road map into their souls. When my earliest encounters with clients are all about big-picture matters — timetables, budgets, contractor choices — I know that I'm going to need to find a way to learn what ignites their passion and animates them in some way. I'll often interrupt a discussion with clients on some very practical matter and intentionally change the subject to art, travel, or some other subject that will clue me in to what it is they love. It may seem to them like a digression, but to me, gaining such insight is essential.

Taking the time to walk through galleries and visit antique dealers, if only to see what a client really connects to, can be time very well spent, even if nothing gets bought. I will often invite clients to visit me in Paris and just *walk* with me. The mere act of strolling through a gorgeous, attraction-filled city like that gets them talking and thinking and free-associating in a way that can lead to exactly the kind of insights I need as I come up with my design. Exploring stores and galleries with a client and stumbling onto some great painting or an unusual table, is a fantastic way to jump-start a design plan — it can even spark the birth of a new collection. And just as importantly, it allows the client to assume emotional ownership of a design that may very well, in those early stages, only exist on paper.

Given that young collections can take time to develop into established ones and that even established collections require space to grow bigger, I factor in the future need for added space in every design. My interiors are tailored to allow the owners maximum freedom to move in whatever direction they might choose. If in a few years' time they decide that their decades-old love affair with American landscape paintings has taken a backseat to a fervid new interest in modern photography, I want them to be able to indulge this new passion without having to rebuild their interiors. By sticking to sound architectural precepts and carefully selecting finishes and furnishings so that they project an aura of timelessness, you can create rooms that don't simply *allow* for such change but actually welcome it.

The flip side of the collector's passion is that without the regular opportunity to shift contexts or alter circumstances, she can stop *seeing* the things she loves. No one is immune to the desensitization that can come from living in the same space and seeing the same things day after day over the course of many years. Moving from one home to another is certainly one great way to shake things up and reconnect with — or perhaps even rethink — your love for the objects around you. But there are less dramatic ways to achieve that same effect and put new energy into your home.

Take me, for example. Since we all tend to use some rooms more than others, I've been known to switch paintings or collectibles from room to room every once in a while. I like the way it forces me to look at things anew and appreciate objects that might otherwise have gotten "lost" through overfamiliarity. Many of my clients are surprised to hear me admit this, given the great pains I take to position every element in their homes just so. But seriously, why not? As I have touched on earlier, it is a great way to reenergize a space and all the things within it. You don't have to move. Just move things *around*.

The Architecture of **Yoshio Taniguchi**

Strong Women, Beautiful Men

Japonisme

banizm

THE ART OF **JAPANESE PRINTS** RICHARD

Sotheby's

The Japanese

MARTIN PURYEAR

INSPIRATION

Inspiration is the most mysterious

aspect of any creative person's process. It can't be forced; it arrives on its own terms, at a time and place of its own choosing. And it doesn't always announce itself immediately. Sometimes it lands softly in your psyche, like a sparrow on a windowsill, and contents itself to wait there patiently for weeks, months, or even years until such time as you're prepared to recognize it and make something out of it.

Many years ago, I was working on some dining-chair designs for a project in New York. I had already come up with the strong but very basic form of a chair, the prototype for which had been sitting in my office for weeks while I tried — in vain — to add something special and unique to its simple silhouette. Somewhat frustrated, I decided to take solace in one of my favorite places: the Metropolitan Museum of Art. I bought myself a ticket to see a retrospective honoring Christian Dior, the fashion icon. So taken was I by the level of minute detail in his work that I made a series of sketches in my notebook, thinking to myself that maybe some of his concepts could translate into drapery or fabric ideas to be used later.

Soon after returning to my office in Washington, I found myself staring once again at the simple chair frame, now practically taunting me in its incompleteness. I pulled out my notebook and came upon a sketch I'd made during my walk through the Dior exhibit: a corset detail with a bit of ribbon lacing running up the back. Staring at the open back of my wooden chair, I grabbed the first piece of string I could get my hands on and criss-crossed it over the frame. *Voilà.* I had my design.

One of the most well-received designs in my Baker furniture collection owes its success to a similar chance encounter. I had been playing with various ideas for a large, round mirror, and after the requisite period of trial and error, I was finally content with the design I'd submitted for production. Soon thereafter, I happened to be visiting Paris, and while walking to dinner one evening I came upon a large antique brooch displayed in the window of a shop on rue Bonaparte. It was a large stone surrounded by a cluster of smaller ones that radiated outward from the center in something like a sunburst pattern. My immediate thought was, *This would make a fantastic mirror!* The very next day I managed to take the design I'd seen on this four-inch piece of jewelry and modify it in order to create a truly spectacular forty-eight-inch wall piece.

Inspiration can come from anywhere. My iPhone is loaded with pictures that I've taken during my morning walks in my neighborhood, stored side by side with images from around the world. When I'm traveling, I especially love to visit historic buildings and museums that show period rooms — spaces that are true to their time. While I have no desire to live in one — or, for that matter, to reproduce one — there's plenty of inspiration to be found in them. Even though they reflect a bygone era, they offer wonderful lessons in proportion, color, furniture, and art. What's true for historians is true for designers as well: the better you understand the past, the more prepared you are to shape the future.

But it bears repeating: inspiration is not imitation. It's not simply about re-creating something you've seen. It's about taking something you've experienced and filtering it through your own private and unique sensibility, so that when it comes out, it comes out new. I think of the process in the same way that a translator of poems must think of his or her source material. A direct, word-for-word translation might be truer to the original poem, but it probably wouldn't be very good. The responsibility of the inspired designer, like that of the translator, is to create an entirely new work that's inextricably linked to the source of inspiration. But the key words in that description are these: *entirely new.*

Reproducing the design of a beautiful chair that you spied at a flea market one day may be commercially savvy, but it isn't inspiration. Inspiration is when you see the chair at the flea market, are struck by some particular aspect of it, and can't get the image of the chair out of your head for weeks. Then one day, you're sitting at your drafting table without a particular goal in mind — just visually free-associating, perhaps — and that one memorable aspect of the flea-market chair suddenly shows up in a spontaneous drawing of a completely *different chair*. The scale is changed, as are the details, but there's no mistaking the source. Just as there's no mistaking that the new chair is an original design.

Practically everything I make, from individual furnishings to entire home interiors, can be traced back to something I saw or experienced that affected me in some way: a garden, a piece of jewelry, a swath of beautiful fabric, a painting, a sculpture, a supremely comfortable chair, a dream, a memory from childhood. But if it's true that potential inspiration is to be found everywhere, it's not equally true that it's always easy to find. The key is to be open-minded, observant...and patient. Let it come to you, and stay in you, for as long as it needs to. Then, when it finally decides to emerge, it will be different. You'll be different, too.

Throughout this book, I have strategically placed a number of my own photographs taken over many recent years of travel. These images are meant to share with you not only those places and elements I find inspirational but also how I "see" them — to be more direct, how I use the lens to edit out that which my eye feels is not important, enabling me to focus on that which I find beautiful. It is through these experiences behind the camera that I have learned to look at my own work and challenge myself to edit and refine. As you look through the pages of my inspirational photos, take a moment and contemplate each image. I hope that you will find a connection to those elements that have inspired me and see how I have incorporated these elements into my own process of creating. In the chapters ahead, "*The Garden,*" "*Paris,*" "*New York,*" and "*Classical Evolution,*" I have taken four different projects and shared my process of using inspiration to assist me in fulfilling these interiors. Though each of these projects presented a unique set of circumstances and challenges, each gave me the opportunity to push myself creatively while remaining true to my process and my love for serenity.

Arcade Table | THOMAS PHEASANT COLLECTION FOR BAKER 2012

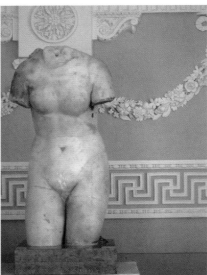

There is a human connection and appreciation to the classical ideals of form and proportion that reach back to our most ancient cultures. Understanding these ideals allows us to work within any architectural style. It is through observation and exposure to the best works of the past that we are able to conceive the best works of the future.

Athens Chair | THOMAS PHEASANT COLLECTION FOR BAKER 2012

The circle has long been recognized as the most perfect
of all forms. It has the power to unify and bring focus...it is
an element that allows the eye to rest while projecting
an ethereal grace.

Helix Mirror | THOMAS PHEASANT STUDIO 2009

There is a necessary confidence required to design with an
eye toward simplicity. It has been through observation that
I have learned to appreciate the beauty of allowing form to
fulfill the design. As my own work evolves, I strive to focus
on only that which is essential. It is an ongoing process
of refinement.

I have always found great beauty in the collaboration between man and the garden. As someone who has spent countless hours attempting to control nature's instincts to wander, I can only admit to being humbled by its force yet persistent in my optimism.

THE GARDEN

I will never forget

the day I received a certain phone call from a very special client.

She was calling me on a cell phone from inside her car, where she sat gazing up at a wonderful house in Southampton. Over the course of several years, I had walked with her and her husband through a number of homes in the Hamptons in hopes of finding the perfect one for them to purchase. But there was always something not quite right with each one we visited: too modern, too big, too small, too far from town, too close to town...you get the idea.

So when I heard her telling me that she was parked in front of the most beautiful house of the entire lot, I was all ears. So taken was she by the facade and gardens. She confessed that she was actually afraid to go inside and be — once again — deterred by an interior that didn't live up to her expectations. I told her to go inside anyway and to call me back once her tour was completed.

As I waited for the phone to ring again, I thought about all the afternoons we had spent together viewing homes. Not once had she ever spoken of any of the houses we'd visited in romantic terms. That's not to say that we didn't see some amazing properties. But this was the first time I had ever heard her admit to having made an immediate emotional connection to a house.

She called me back. Of course, her fears had been realized: this early-1900s home, so beautiful on the outside, was on the inside a jumble of disconnected moments, a chaotic patchwork of competing vestiges from past renovations. Antique French paneling had been installed in the living room back in the 1950s; a Georgian library appeared to have remained untouched since its emergence in the 1970s; a large dining room had been stripped of all its original details sometime during the 1990s; the second and third floors were little more than an endless-seeming sequence of bedrooms with little charm and fewer closets.

As she expressed her disappointment to me, somewhat curiously, she kept interrupting herself with a repeated phrase: "But the outside is *so wonderful.*" I took it as a cue. By the end of our phone conversation, we decided that it was worth my coming up to Southampton and taking a look for myself.

When I arrived at the house, I instantly saw what she had fallen in love with; I, too, found myself being swept away. This amazing Shingle Style home, with its beautifully appointed details articulated in glossy ivory paint, was surrounded by lush and expansive gardens filled with roses, hydrangea and boxwood. When I stepped inside to tour the interior, I noticed how strongly I was drawn to the views outside each window. As distressed as the interiors were, it was easy

for me to imagine how they must have (or at least *should* have) looked long ago. The residence was whispering in my ear, good-naturedly challenging me. It was posing my favorite kind of question: How could I borrow the language of its facade and gardens and combine it with the vocabulary of the original architecture in order to create a new interior language — one that, once fully articulated, would appear to be not of this moment but integrally and essentially *of this house*?

Before I exited the property, I took dozens of photographs of the exterior. I wandered the outside and studied the garden, admiring the tidily clipped boxwood and the old wisteria that had somehow managed to survive multiple generations. On the plane back to Washington, I reviewed the existing floor plans and made endless notes, cataloging my first impressions. By the time my plane had landed — and New York to D.C. is a short flight — I was convinced that this was the house.

A few conversations with my clients was enough to convince them that I could take the existing interior and transform it into a seamless reflection of the exterior. I have to say, their faith in my stated confidence was remarkable, given the investment they would be making. I was reminded, humbly, how faith of that sort is precisely what motivates and empowers me to take on formidable tasks — and, in carrying them out, to reach down as deeply as I can into my creative vault.

The first efforts all focused on flow: putting together a new floor plan within the confines of the home's existing footprint. A new center hall was created; door openings were relocated to maximize views to the outside; the trail of tiny bedrooms was reconfigured to allow for a large master suite and comfortable guest rooms; kitchens, baths, and closets were all expanded to suit the practical needs of its modern owners. Once the floor plan had been established, I began working on building the interior vocabulary of distinguishing architectural details. As it turned out, to come up with that vocabulary all I had to do was look outside; almost every inspiration I could ever hope to find was right there, either set into the silvery-taupe shingle facade surrounding the front door or popping out at me in the amazing garden.

As I began sketching details, I first focused on the dining room. This particular space was at the core of the house's main floor, with its two large bays of French doors that linked it to the rose garden on one side and the pool terrace on the other. Where better to begin the process of bringing the garden inside? My sketches were a series of elevations using details inspired by the notion of an indoor gazebo. I had always admired the French use of treillage, although I had never before introduced it into any of my work. Visiting the site one day, I noticed that on either side of each dining bay were a pair of tall white dogwood trees that, over time, had grown large enough so that their branches caressed the outside of each bay. I immediately began to sketch a ceiling detail with curling dogwood branches punctuated by large white blossoms.

> "A special magic happens when
> a house opens up to nature."

It was a moment of instant inspiration. When I presented my ideas for this space to the client, however, she wasn't nearly as taken with the idea. Her lukewarm response didn't represent a lack of faith in me, she assured, but nevertheless it was very difficult for her to visualize this idea, just conceptually speaking. But I was gently insistent and, ultimately, persuasive. She so loved my idea of transforming the dining room into a "gazebo" of white plaster that she was willing to take a chance by indulging me in my excitement over the decorative branch-and-blossom motif on the ceiling.

I am extraordinarily fortunate to have so many clients who place their trust completely in me and my creative process, but of course there are times when one of my proposals is met with a less than enthusiastic response of the sort I was met with initially. Knowing just when to push and just when to let go of an idea can be one of the trickier aspects of the kind of work I do. Still, when I'm absolutely one hundred percent confident that a new idea will have a great outcome...well, this is when I'm willing to take the risk. And this was definitely one of those moments.

Throughout the many months of renovation, we employed a number of wonderful artisans who helped me fulfill my plan for this house. But none of my positive experiences with any of them could have prepared me for what awaited me on the day I came up to Southampton to supervise installation of the plaster relief along the dining room ceiling.

Long before my visit, I had sent the contractor a series of drawings articulating my overall vision for an application of stylized branches which I had hoped — and which I had promised my clients — would translate into a graceful, stunningly beautiful design. My draftsmen had worked from multiple photographs of dogwood trees to help them generate the most realistic studies possible for modeling the plaster. As I entered the dining room that day, the plasterers had created no fewer than two hundred *unique* dogwood blossoms, each of them at a different stage of development, from bud to full blossom. A table that ran the full length of the dining room displayed rows of pure white blossoms, each one indisputably its own distinct work of art.

My branches had already been installed along the plaster ceiling. One of the artisans stood on top of a mini-scaffold and patiently waited as I

handed him one gorgeous, perfect blossom after another, directing its exact placement. Each of the flowers found a home in just the right position along the scrolling white branches. It will live forever in my memory as a unique triumph for the collective creative process, from concept to implementation. The artisans who had labored so intensely on these delicate botanical elements had understood, intuitively, what I was after and delivered in a way that had exceeded my wildest expectations. That alone counted as a rewarding experience. But the sense of reward was increased exponentially when my clients saw what we had done and expressed their immediate and deeply felt love for it.

Quietly, I returned to the garden for more inspiration. I found that I was able to fold the ideas it so generously bestowed upon me into each room of the house, appointing different spaces with appropriately proportioned trim, paneling, crowns, and bases that borrowed from its forms. I kept searching for and finding new ways to take traditional ideas and infuse them with subtle but surprising connections to the landscape. Where dentil moldings might have been the expected solution, for instance, I installed delicate bands of fretwork. Furnishings received similar treatment. Custom rugs were designed in various patterns that incorporated leaf, branch, and flower details; draperies were emblazoned with embroidered borders of flowers and more fretwork. The mosaic tile floors brought together other garden elements, and in doing so they added a distinctive yet thematically related charm to each of the baths.

Once it was fully established, the interior palette beautifully echoed the manner in which the exterior palette's ivory and silver tones gave way to the lush, vibrant colors of the garden. A highly organized system of quiet neutrals on walls and furniture eased the eye's path toward windows, where views of the magnificent garden provided spectacular bursts of chromatic energy.

I love to be in this house and slowly take in the full effect of gazing across these softly colored interiors through windows that, to me, appear almost as frames for some of the most vivid landscape paintings I have ever encountered. It's the ideal way to experience a house that has always been known — and, for the foreseeable future, will continue to be known — as Gardenside.

Garden details subtly worked their way into the furnishings and architectural details of this Southampton residence to give the house its unique connection to the garden. *At right and below,* custom floral carpet designs and drapery panels embroidered with lattice borders in soft neutral tones yield to the lush garden views outside every window.

"There is nothing more humbling than the moments of wonder found within the walls of a garden."

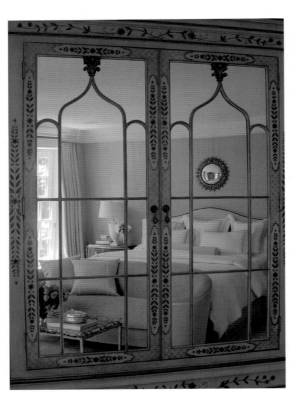

PARIS

Over a decade ago,

during a short getaway to Paris, my partner and I walked into a real estate office and inquired about available apartments on the Left Bank. We did this with absolutely no intention of buying an apartment but solely out of curiosity. We had walked past a few real estate offices that day, all with photographs of dream spaces plastered in their windows. When I passed each window, I would scan each photo imagining how I would transform each empty space. That afternoon, during a very long and luxurious lunch, we talked of how wonderful it would be to have an apartment in this amazing city and perhaps one day, in the distant future, spend less time working and more time traveling. As we left the restaurant, I noticed yet another real estate office just across the street.

Without hesitation, we walked into the office and asked a young lady sitting at the front desk if she knew of any apartments available in the area. Like any good agent, she asked us what exactly were we looking for. When I responded that we were interested in a two-bedroom with great views that required little work, she replied without hesitation, "This is what all you Americans want. I am sorry, but I do not have anything to show you." Not sure exactly how to reply, I meekly passed her my card and asked her to contact me if something came up.

We left the office and quickly dismissed any thoughts of apartments as our focus turned immediately to the beautiful shops and magical views of the Seine as the sun lowered itself on the edge of the city. Later that day when we returned to our hotel we had a

message on the answering machine. It was the young woman from the real estate office. She left a brief message stating that an apartment had just become available on Boulevard Saint Germain. She proposed that we meet her the next day at 2:00 p.m., otherwise she would be showing it to someone else. On an impulse, I called her back and agreed to meet her at exactly 2:00.

The next day as we walked to meet her, we laughed about our entertaining the idea of an apartment in Paris. There was no way we were prepared to indulge ourselves into such a big commitment. We were there strictly out of curiosity and the fun of exploring the inside of one of Baron Haussmann's lovely apartment facades. As we approached the building, my laughter was dimmed by a sudden sense of attraction. I stared up at the limestone facade with its black iron railings looking onto the wide boulevard and thought, *If I were going to take an apartment in Paris, this would be the kind of building I would look for.* For most of us, it is the rebuilding of Paris under the direction of Haussmann that has created the Paris we know today. While scholars have debated the positive and negative impact of his vision, you cannot walk the streets of this city and not credit him with masterminding what has become one of the most beautiful urban environments in the world. Speaking for myself, I have always been enthralled by the absolute purity and unyielding clarity of that vision. Where some others might find in Paris's stately and handsome blocks a stolid sameness, I find a beautiful rhythm. In his

design for the city, Haussmann exorcised all traces of urban chaos and replaced it with tranquil order.

These, of course, are the same design goals I have set for my interiors. Naturally, I was curious to see whether these goals could have been met on the inside of a typically Parisian apartment building as successfully as they had been met on the outside. And now I was about to find out.

The front door opened, and the agent waved us into a small courtyard where we found the entrance into the building. As we entered into a small elevator, I could not help but imagine life in such a building. The elevator stopped at the fourth floor, and we walked up to a pair of dark lacquered doors. As the agent opened the doors to the empty apartment, my excitement was shot down immediately by a white laminate storage closet that was nailed to a plaster wall in the foyer and the sight of exposed water pipes that ran across the outside corners of the space. This is not the apartment I had just imagined only thirty seconds earlier. As I glanced to my left, there was a large pair of French windows that looked out across the most beautiful cityscape. The apartment was perched high enough to allow a clear shot across the city to an iconic view of Sacré-Coeur in the far distance. It looked as if Disney had created this Parisian view for one of its animated films. As we proceeded through the apartment room by room, it began to open up and reveal beautiful nineteenth-century details.

The palette of my Paris apartment is a direct reflection of the city just outside each window. *At left,* inspired by the streets lined in pale limestone facades, accented in black iron, and punctuated by carefully pruned trees, I have turned Paris outside in. Throughout the day, as the light of the city changes, so does the atmosphere inside my apartment. It has been a fascinating study in the interaction of color and light.

"It has been an exciting process of infusing my American style into a space I wanted to remain totally French."

My mind was racing. Could I have an apartment in Paris? How can I be serious about the first apartment I have seen? How would I go about renovating and furnishing it long-distance? Most importantly, once finished, would I ever have time to visit?

After our tour, the agent told us that she was late for another appointment and that we could stay and lock the door when we were ready to leave. For the next few hours, I walked the apartment thinking of how I would go about rebuilding the space for us. In just a few hours, my thoughts had moved from curious tourist to *I want this apartment!* Over the next few weeks, we flew back and forth from D.C. to Paris, working with lawyers, interviewing contractors, opening bank accounts, and making appointments to see a slew of other apartments that only confirmed my initial thoughts that this was the right apartment for us.

Within three months, we had completed plans for the apartment renovation and hired a contractor to begin the work. Designing the apartment was easy. Using the elements that Baron Haussmann had already laid out before me, I took my inspiration from the boulevard just outside my windows. The pale shades of the limestone facades accented by gray slate roofs and black ornamental railings provided me with a perfect palette.

Taking a light hand with the furniture, I fabricated the upholstery and carpets in pale shades of gray and had them shipped from my workrooms in the United States. I also designed several special pieces for the apartment. Among the custom pieces was a black lacquered game table and a large glass-and-lacquer folding screen designed to bring a modern energy to the pale neutral palette. Plaster ceilings and panel moldings that were original to the apartment were found in the existing living room and dining room. These surviving details became the foundation for my renovation process. The bathrooms, hall, and bedrooms had been stripped of their original details, but these spaces were full of light and were easily detailed in the spirit of the nineteenth century.

During the course of the renovation, I slowly acquired light fixtures, art, and objects from various dealers along the Left Bank. These pieces, along with the Parisian details incorporated into the plaster and moldings, set the tone for an apartment that we would soon consider being one of the best decisions of our life. Most importantly, when I step into the apartment, there is no question that I am in the heart of Paris.

"I took my inspiration from the wide
boulevard just outside my windows."

The balcony off our living room offers a panoramic view of the tree-lined boulevard with its designer shops, patisseries, and restaurants. Florists, chocolatiers, and antique dealers present window displays that tempt and inspire. It is impossible to walk for more that one block in any direction and not be taken by the creative spirit and care of presentation that is displayed in the windows of the various shops and galleries.

The first evening of every trip begins with a long walk through the side streets that house the many famed art and antique dealers of the Left Bank. We take our time, stopping frequently to look into each window in hopes of finding that special object that will launch an idea or become the special focus for a new project.

As I write this book, it has been ten years since that moment when we first stepped foot into this apartment. It has been an amazing adventure that continues to this day. My time in Paris has taught me first and foremost to appreciate the value of slower days and what the French poet Charles Baudelaire called *un flâneur* — someone perfectly content to walk every mile of this beautiful city with no specific destination in mind, and who experiences it far more fully, precisely because of this rapturous, unfocused freedom. Every day I spend wandering its streets, Paris offers me another opportunity to discover entirely new ways of looking at the world and time to contemplate the future course of my own creativity.

I have come to know Paris very well and have made a number of dear friends that have opened the city to me in ways that I could never have imagined on that fortuitous day ten years ago, when I innocently asked a lovely French girl if she knew of any apartments that happened to be available in the neighborhood.

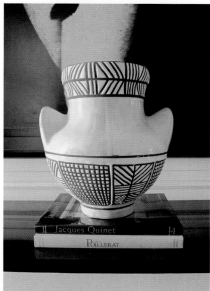

NEW YORK

When clients approached me

255

to ask if I would have time to take on a new project for them in New York, I responded yes without hesitation. I had worked with them on their Georgetown residence a few years before and had enjoyed the luxury of working for these wonderful people and their joy for creating a beautiful home. They were interested in a small pied-à-terre in New York that would provide them a comfortable place to stay during visits for business and family get-togethers.

Within a few days, we were walking through a small apartment located on Central Park South discussing the possibilities of turning it into something that might suit their needs. A perfect location, it contained adequate square footage with windows that looked out on what could be considered pleasant city views. During the walk-through, one of my clients turned to the agent and asked if there were any other apartments available in the building. He mentioned that there was one on an upper floor with great views of the park, but it occupied the whole floor.

Surprisingly, they asked if we could take a look. A few minutes later, were walking into a space that was totally and completely vacant, devoid not only of decor or finishes but of any interior walls; it was just rambling open space contained by twin expanses of concrete that

made up the floor and ceiling. Along the entire length of the apartment, the walls were punctuated by a long row of large windows all looking out to the most amazing views of Central Park. As I approached the windows, I was instantly taken by the breadth of the park and the rows of iconic buildings along the east and west sides that contain this verdant urban oasis.

It was so post card perfect that I could only compare it to the movies of the 1940s that depicted modern living in Manhattan. I imagined interiors designed for Rosalind Russell, Cary Grant, and Lauren Bacall — those amazing midcentury highly polished interiors that somehow rose above the hectic city below and were occupied by only glamorous people wearing beautiful clothes. I wandered through this empty unit imagining the creation of a floating space that would detach itself from noise and traffic. By the time I had walked the entire space, I was already visualizing what could be.

Returning to Washington, D.C., my clients and I weighed the different possibilities afforded by both apartments. I tried to set aside my preference for the larger of the two units we had seen; the decision, after all, was theirs and theirs alone to make. The difference between the two spaces

was significant, but that meant only that two equally different design approaches were called for, depending on whatever choice they ultimately made. Either apartment presented a great opportunity to create something new and wonderful for them.

A few days later, my clients called to tell me that they had decided to purchase the larger unit and that they wanted me to begin the design process as soon as possible. Needless to say, I was thrilled. In short order, I was back in New York, once again walking through this remarkable space with my staff in tow. We photographed and measured every inch of its authentically blank slate. I found, perhaps unsurprisingly, that I could not keep myself away from that spectacular row of windows that so profoundly connected this undeveloped volume to the highly developed cityscape on the other side of its walls.

Having a vivid imagination is a fantastic tool, but it is often tempered by reality. As I entered the unit during this second visit, I noticed that there was a large steel beam that ran the entire length of the space. Not only did it divide the entire space down the middle, it also dropped from the ceiling approximately two feet. Suddenly, my creative flow was shut down by an element that would present an unavoidable roadblock.

ART + ARCHITECTURE

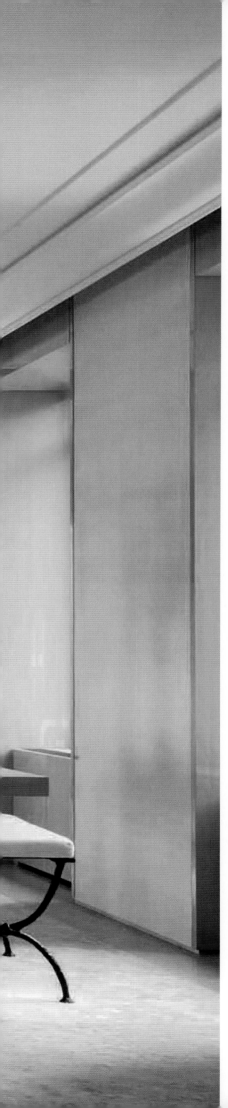

"I imagined an urban oasis
high above the noise and traffic."

I would spend the next few weeks studying the floor plan and playing with ideas that would incorporate this beam in a way that would make it disappear. I would eventually come up with the idea of fabricating a chain of wooden boxes that would become transitions into each living space of the apartment. These boxes would visually frame the entry into each room and push the living areas toward the windows along the park. These wooden transitions would become a repeated element throughout the apartment; sometimes they would be used as transitions into open spaces, and other times I would use them as internal passages that allowed us to create intimate spaces to link guest rooms and the master suite to the main living areas. It would also become the treatment used for the elevator lobby that would immediately set the tone as you entered the residence. The roadblock turned into an asset. The wooden passages whose heights were limited to nine feet worked to enhance the feeling of air as you moved into the living spaces whose ceilings rose to eleven feet. Once the floor plan was in place and the solutions for concealing beams and HVAC and electrical were well underway, my focus turned back to my initial thoughts of a serene interior floating above the park.

Meanwhile, my clients began to think and talk about how they planned to live in their new apartment. Their home in Washington, D.C., was an historic Georgetown residence that we had completely rebuilt and furnished with a mix of English antiques and classic, simple upholstery. The interiors had been inspired by traditional Georgian architecture and designed around the couple's growing collection of nineteenth-century French paintings whose colors had helped direct the chromatic program for most of the house. But now, in Manhattan, they wanted to move in an entirely different direction. They shared with me their interest in using the new apartment to showcase a collection of contemporary art — a collection that had existed only in their hopes and dreams at that stage, insofar as they had yet to acquire any actual artworks. To them, the New York residence represented an opportunity to create and live in a modern setting that would provide a bold counterpoint to their life in D.C.

263

"When I returned, the apartment had taken on the dynamic works of artists such as Hoffman, Léger, Judd, Arp...yet it maintained its ethereal quality."

By this point, it was clear to me that my clients had moved well beyond thinking of this apartment as a simple pied-à-terre to call home during occasional visits to New York City. They were genuinely and visibly thrilled at the thought of inhabiting a totally different environment and drawing upon a totally different kind of energy. Like me, they had looked out the windows during our initial walk-through and witnessed an intoxicating vision of urbanity and sophistication. Now they were taking the exciting step of actually inserting themselves into the vision: grandly opening the curtains, just as Cary Grant or Lauren Bacall might have, and greeting the sparkling city below.

I kept this image in mind as I began considering finishes, colors, and furnishings. Often a client's collections will drive certain decisions in my design process, and this couple's Georgetown residence was a good example. But given that their collection of contemporary art didn't exist yet, I found myself in the somewhat unusual position of drawing inspiration from a purely theoretical source. I had to envision an interior that celebrated the incredible view but also didn't overpower the impact of a yet-to-be-defined art collection. At the same time, I was also aware that it would probably take a while for my clients to acquire enough of a collection to fill a space of this size. My goal, then, became to design a home for them that could be equally fulfilling with or without the introduction of brilliant paintings and sculptures. I wanted to give them the chance to live in a simply beautiful apartment, one that could live up

to that description regardless of any masterpieces that might one day be housed within it.

As I worked out the design vocabulary for the apartment, I connected to my first thoughts of those Hollywood film sets of the 1940s. While I am not at all interested in replicating a midcentury movie set, there is a certain quality to these interiors that I have always appreciated. Perhaps it is the luxurious simplicity that flows effortlessly through each room. never revealing the calculated energy put into each and every detail.

This apartment was completed a few years ago and was presented to my clients with the walls completely free of any artworks. The simple serenity of the interior and the careful use of beautiful materials accomplished my goal. When I returned this year to photograph it for this book, I entered into an apartment that had evolved. The interior had taken on the dynamic works of artists such as Hoffman, Léger, Judd, Arp, and many others. Through this new collection, present to me as I reentered their home, I was given new insight into the current passions of the people who had given me such freedom to guide them through the creation of their new home.

And yet as I walked the apartment, I was delighted to feel that this home high above the park, while evolving in the hands of my dear clients, had maintained its ethereal quality gently hovering above the urban life just outside those beautiful windows...with plenty of space to breathe.

There is an energy that is unique to New York. I wanted to bring that energy inside while maintaining a mood of serenity high above this dynamic city. *At left and above,* through the geometric rhythm of the design, I was able to create a strong architectural vocabulary that directs and organizes the apartment into simple vertical and horizontal planes. While my primary focus was to guide the eye toward the windows that look out onto amazing city views, I was also using my architectural elements to bring a dynamic focus to my client's future collections.

CLASSICAL EVOLUTION

Portico of the National Gallery of Art | WASHINGTON, D.C. 2011

What project could

possibly reveal more about me than my own home? In truth, I could live in any number of houses or apartments that offer me inspiration and enough room to create. My current home in Washington, D.C., is a result of an off-and-on focus to find a house that would allow my partner and I space to work at home on the weekends and have out-of-town guests come and go without any impact on our daily routine. My instructions to the real estate agent were firm; find us an old house in need of renovation that had enough space for a library and at least two guest rooms. I also mentioned that since we traveled so much, we did not want the responsibilities of a large garden, and a pool was absolutely out of the question.

My true motivation was that my partner and I had been living in the same home for twenty years. It was a charming gatehouse located in the center of Georgetown – a small Italianate two-bedroom cottage that was surrounded by stucco walls and a storybook garden. When we first saw the property, it had been abandoned and overgrown. As I stepped through its gates into what felt like a private world, I immediately imagined its potential. The creative thoughts flowed through me so fast that even before I concluded our tour of this crumbling house, I had decided that we must have it. We indeed purchased it, but with the idea of developing the property and selling it for profit.

What actually happened was that a year later, after going through months of developing the house and grounds, we fell in love with it. We moved in with the idea that it would be for a year or two until we found a larger home. Now twenty years later, it was time for a change.

For two years, we had looked at a number of nice properties without ever really feeling the urge to purchase. Nothing matched the romantic charm of our tiny cottage. One day, we received a call from our very patient real estate agent telling us to go see a house. She gave us the address, and we immediately drove over to see it. The house was just ten years old and sitting on a large piece of land. The facade was simple and well-proportioned, and I could tell by the walls that surrounded the property that this was much more property than we wanted to take on. Also, the fact that it was a relatively new house did not push my romantic button. I reluctantly entered the house convinced this was just another fruitless house tour.

As I entered the front door, I could catch glimpses of exterior views and I was struck by the sense of space. The formal interior had been carefully planned and detailed in a fashion that did not reflect my personal style, but I could immediately begin imagining the possibilities of a new interior. As I walked through the first floor, I noticed that many of the entertaining rooms were visually cut off from the views of the property. The rooms were formally appointed and provided comfortable moments of intimacy. The windows were small and heavily draped, keeping all the focus inside. Here was a house that was beautifully done for someone else, yet just as during that first visit to the small Georgetown cottage, I was able to cut through what existed to envision what *could be*.

As I peered out of the small windows of the living room to the garden and pool, all of my former demands of no pool and no large

garden were forgotten. My focus turned to the idea of opening up the spaces on the first floor to allow a direct view to the pool. I quickly imagined a more formal garden with clipped hedges and new pool house that would provide a classical backdrop for the large windows that I would install along the east side of the house. As I stood gazing out at the property, I could see that this house could provide us with all the privacy of our Georgetown cottage while being an opportunity to work within a bigger volume of space and to exercise my love for modern classical style.

It took eighteen months to turn this property into the home I had imagined on that first reluctant visit. As it is with most projects, it was those first hours of walking through the space that I found most exciting. I have learned that it is impossible to list what will touch my creative nerve. Any house or apartment can provide an opportunity to be creative, but some spark an immediate flow of ideas and an ease of direction. It is very much like the relationships we develop with people. You meet many lovely people along the way, but every now and then you meet someone special that you connect with, and the relationship flows naturally. For me, houses offer the same connection.

I remember pushing through the plans and elevations of our new home quickly and with great confidence. My goal was to simplify the house and reduce its formality while maintaining a connection to classical ideas. I wanted a modern house that would be full of light and air, a house that would reflect my personal vision of modern classical style, and a home that would afford us a private oasis in the middle of the city.

"Understanding the past is the first step in moving forward."

First, rooms were combined to offer larger, more open spaces. All of the entertaining spaces were reworked to focus attention toward the pool and fill the house with light. The former architectural details were stripped, and gone were the pairs of columns that greeted you as you entered. Windows were enlarged and door openings reoriented and heightened to present a new, bolder scale. Marble floors and stenciled paneling were all removed and replaced with limestone blocks and crisply painted moldings accented with dark mahogany-paneled doors. The four bedrooms upstairs were redesigned into two guest rooms and a larger master suite. The master bedroom and bath would now look over the pool and into the most private views of the garden, allowing me to keep my windows always open to the views without concern for privacy.

But the most exciting space was found in the lower level. Formerly designed as a game room with a large bar and pool table, here I was able to transform it into a new space that would allow me to surround myself with my books and provide a luxury I had only dreamed about: a place to work at home whenever I felt the urge. It is also the room that I refer to as *the balance room*. It is that room within a house that offers you alternative emotional nourishment. In my home, I have designed the rooms around a light neutral palette with windows that pull in the sun and the outdoors. In my new library, or balance room, I have created a space that is rich in the deep tones of espresso with dark linen walls and bookcases detailed in dark mahogany. The result is a room that pulls you inside and allows a different type of nurturing. It is a room that allows me to turn off the outside and focus within a space that surrounds you like a blanket.

Next, all attention was directed to the property just outside that would soon become the focus of the new interiors. The existing pool was perfectly located and only required new resurfacing and stone. The existing pool house would require more thought. Like most renovations, there are always those surprises that require enlarging the scope of the project. My original thoughts were to simply change the facade by adding larger glass doors and replacing light fixtures. Once we began exploring the conditions of the pool house, I decided it was best to enlarge the scope of the work and rethink the function and the importance of this facade. Working within the footprint, only the existing terra-cotta roof

would remain. The new plan would call for an interior space that would open up not only to the pool but also to a private dining terrace off to the side. This dining terrace would be surrounded by a tall hedge and offer a surprise element to the garden. The landscape would now become not just a green background but it's own architectural element. Trees pruned into aerial hedges channel you through the garden along limestone paths. Just as I simplified the interior, I wanted the garden to reflect an elegant simplicity. I limited the varieties of plants and trees and restricted the hardscape to limestone and stucco in a unified palette.

As soon as the house plans and landscape details were completed, I turned my attention back to the interiors. Now was the time to focus on decoration and furnishings. I wanted the furniture to reflect and support the vocabulary of the new architecture. After all, here was the perfect opportunity to create unique furnishings that would rest within my newly planned spaces. Just as I had looked to modernize the classical elements of the house itself, I decided to begin by designing one new piece of furniture for each room. These new designs would launch each room interior and allow me to push myself freely to experiment with classical forms and materials. Mahogany and bronze became the common elements for these new pieces. An oval center table for the living room, a pair of column-based tables with limestone tops for the foyer, and a hall cabinet with woven bronze doors would come together and ignite the spirit of this new collection. Next, I would introduce ivory leather details into a tall cabinet for the master bedroom; cast bronze details in organic textures would appear on the hardware and take the form of capitals on columns for a console on the second floor.

As the renovation progressed and the interiors were being developed, I began to look back at my furniture designs from past years. I started to pull in pieces from former collections along with a few pieces I had designed years ago and had placed in storage hoping for just the right project to come along. Soon the construction was completed, and the interiors began to take form. New designs mixed with pieces from the past. Collections from my travels were placed, and artworks that I had acquired over the years took on a new life within the openness of the new spaces.

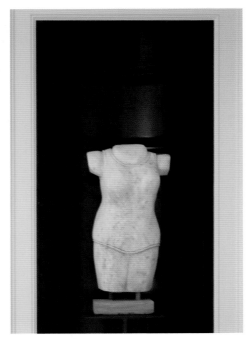

281

"A guest once commented that my home is a kind of Thomas Pheasant retrospective...he was right."

Soon after we moved in, we invited a friend from out of town to come and stay for a few days. After he arrived and was given a quick tour of our new home, he turned to me and said, "This house is a kind of Thomas Pheasant retrospective." He noted that every time he asked about a piece of furniture or light fixture, I responded with, "*I designed that for the house*," or "*I designed that in 1990*," or "*That's from my Baker collection*," or "*That's from my McGuire collection*." Honestly, I had not thought of the house that way, but he was right. This house had become the depository of a long history of design showcasing my personal evolution. What really struck me was how comfortable pieces designed twenty years ago rested with the new pieces I had just designed for this interior.

Without realizing it, I had created a home that reflects who I am and where I have been, and it has the space to contemplate where I am going. Creating for myself has been a truly remarkable process, and each day I reap the rewards of this passionate labor. This is what I hope to provide for my clients, rooms that express who they are and give them comfort to dream of what they may become.

Throughout the interior of the house, I kept consistency in both color palette and materials. *At right and above,* here in the kitchen I continued the use of wall paneling in ivory lacquer that I introduced in the center hall. The limestone floors that are found just outside the kitchen in large blocks were reintroduced in a mosaic pattern. These types of textural changes are needed to keep this type of flow interesting. And just as in the main rooms of the house, I introduced contrast through dark mahogany accents. All of this was done to allow the kitchen to gracefully open up to the rest of the main floor and provide a seamless experience.

At right, originally a very dark space, the lower level was transformed into my library. By opening up the room to the outside and using the crisp contrast of white paint against dark mahogany, I was able to bring a modern energy to the space. Rather than selecting light-colored fabrics and carpets to lighten the room, I chose to introduce dark espresso colors to heighten the contrast of the white paneling. By day, the natural light illuminates the white trim and ceiling to create a surprisingly bright space. In the evening, the white paint softens, and the dark bookcases and furnishings recede into what becomes a rich cocoon that wraps you like a blanket. As much as I enjoy the light fabrics used in the rest of the house, the deep palette of this room gives my home a wonderful balance.

Furniture design has long been a wonderful exploration into creating pieces that house all the elements I use in building my interiors. Throughout my home, I have mixed a variety of my furniture designs from the past twenty years. *At left,* simplicity, sculpture, details, contrast, and my love for bringing the past forward are realized in this unique mahogany and ivory leather cabinet I designed for my bedroom. The lounge chair and small bronze side table are from my Thomas Pheasant for Baker collection. *Above,* a Greek-inspired bench rests comfortably under this black-and-white painting by Caio Fonseca.

PERFECTION

THE MYTH

Inside every true designer, I believe there's an inner voice that is charged with two closely related tasks: to carry you through each project — no matter how exhausting or difficult the path to completion may be — and to push you, all the while, toward perfection.

Any creative act entails risk. But risk is the price we pay for the chance to reap the reward that comes from creating something beautiful and enduring. And even risk can be a welcome component to a creative endeavor. With risk comes excitement and the possibility of happy surprise. My own trustworthy inner voice tells me that it's okay to take risks and helpfully advises me on which decisions are riskier than others. And it never lets up on its other duty: to urge me toward excellence and sublimeness — in other words, toward perfection.

So what *is* perfection, exactly, for a designer? Is it measured by the joy expressed by a happy client or in the discerning eye of an editor? Or does it reside solely within the designer? After all, designing interiors is a subjective art form that, in my world, is created in the mind of one for the use and appreciation of another.

For me, obviously, designing interiors isn't just a job. It's much more like a journey that happily combines adventure, artistic expression, the development of strong personal relationships, and an ongoing process of creative evolution. With every project, I learn something new about design *and* myself; I become not only a better designer but also, I hope, a richer and fuller individual. Whenever I start work on something, it's always with the fervent hope that I'll be able to step up to the next rung of creativity and maybe even satisfy that constant inner voice's quiet demand for perfection. But while I have every confidence in my ability to build beautiful and comforting spaces for my clients, achieving the perfect interior is, unsurprisingly, not a simple matter.

It goes without saying that the specific quality and character of our living environments affect our emotional well-being. Understanding this connection is key to any good designer's approach. In my own approach, I've tried to pay special attention to one particular aspect of this connection: the way that improving our physical, inhabitable spaces can lead to improvements in our inner, emotional spaces. Put another way, I'm interested in exploring

the link between how making changes in our homes can help us feel better about making changes in our own lives — how the evolution of a home can, and very often does, mirror the evolution of a mind or a soul.

I myself sensed this connection very early on as that young boy who found himself standing between the grand columns of the National Gallery, awestruck and silenced by the beauty of what I beheld. It would strike me again just a few years later, whenever I watched one of those amazing Fred Astaire and Ginger Rogers movies where the whole world seemed united in one stylish black-and-white confection, a dreamworld whose carefully edited sets provided such a welcome escape from the not-always-dreamlike reality just outside the sliding doors of my suburban family room.

In moments like these — moments when we truly allow ourselves to be transported into a different realm that's well outside of our everyday world — we are given a wonderful gift: room. Room to imagine and envision our own brighter, more beautiful futures. Another name for this state of mind, I think, is serenity.

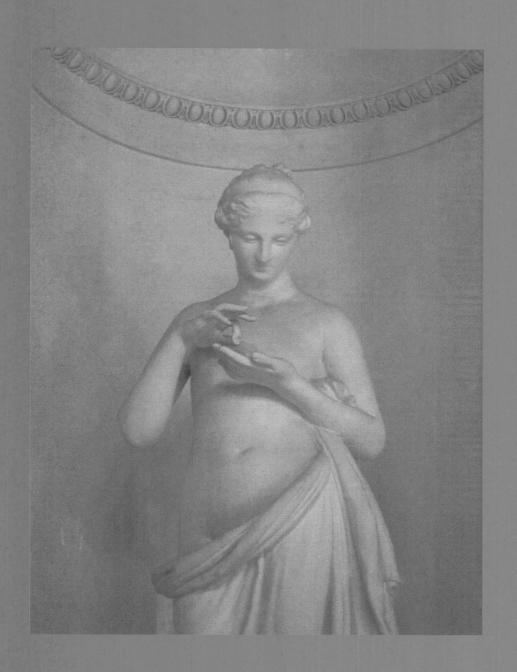

Pavlovsk Palace | ST. PETERSBURG OCTOBER 2012

I concluded long ago that it wasn't the neutral palette or all the classical references that so captured the attention of my clients. What they were responding to, above all else, was this gift: serenity. It's within this serene space that people do their dreaming, and it's where they're best able to summon the strength they may need to lift themselves up, away from whatever stressors or problems may be lingering on the other side of the door.

Throughout my own evolution as a designer, I've tried to go a little easier on myself when I feel like I haven't met my self-imposed threshold of perfection. One reason is that the more I learn, the more I realize there's always *more* to learn. Another reason has to do with the insight that greater joy is often found in the process that has led to a result than in the result itself. Sometimes my clients will suggest to me that they, too, have arrived at this same insight.

But whether I'm making a home for them or a home for myself, I can count on any number of things that will conspire to thwart my goal of achieving perfection. When I'm creating a home for myself, of course, I must assume the dual role of designer *and* client: just as my other clients do, I go through the same sequence of emotions, typically starting with a tremendous rush of optimism and excitement that eventually morphs into something else.

I must balance my vision of what could be with the reality of what *is*: construction delays, cost overruns, and various other unforeseen roadblocks.

Perfection is elusive and never, ever guaranteed. But that's precisely what makes it such an irresistible goal — and not just for me. Once I've completed a project, I do everything I can to help my clients understand their role in maintaining the balance of style and serenity that I've just worked so hard to give them. Some of them who may be expecting me to announce that these spaces must never change are undoubtedly surprised when I tell them the exact opposite. Because no matter how perfect an interior might seem at the moment of completion, to be *truly* perfect — to be the kind of space that nurtures growth and serenity — that interior must be allowed to evolve. Just as people have to adapt to new circumstances and be free to expand their lives, so must their homes be able to accommodate these changes. This inviolable principle is, to me, the essence of modernism. After all, what could be more modern than acknowledging, accepting, and even welcoming change?

We all need room to rest, breathe, and grow. But not just any room will do. My goal is, and has always been, to infuse space with the one quality — serenity — that, more than any

other, encourages and fosters these activities. So how do I know, then, when I've reached perfection? It's when a client tells me that he or she was sitting and relaxing recently in one of my spaces and had a brilliant idea, solved a vexing problem, or made a momentous life decision. That's the most accurate measure I have at my disposal.

When I think back to that grade-school field trip to the National Gallery — when I witness, through the lens of my memory, that boy standing under the rotunda — I see how, at that moment, I was being given the gift that I aspire to pass along to every single one of my clients. Though I'll never know what his specific circumstances were, I can say with absolute certainty that John Russell Pope — the architect of that heavenly space — had been given this same gift at some point during his own journey. His design represented a sincere wish to pass it along. And on that particular day, I was the lucky recipient.

As I continue to design and create — for many more years, I hope — I'm highly aware of this gift's eternal value. To be able to relax in a beautiful and serene space and imagine an exciting future, filled with peace and joy and creation, is to have been given a rare gift indeed. I'm extraordinarily lucky to have received it. I'm even luckier to be allowed to share it with others.

"Perfection
is a motivation,
not a destination."

– Thomas Pheasant

THE REALITY

Many years ago, a friend innocently commented that I was so fortunate to have wonderful clients who have such beautiful homes to work with, and that all I need to do is paint and decorate. While I will admit to the good fortune of having wonderful clients, the rooms and spaces that they present to me are typically far from perfect. It is in the process of working within these "imperfect" rooms that I find the challenge and the joy of designing. The architectural transformation that takes place in these spaces is essential to the overall success of the decorating. As I have stated earlier in the book, beautiful interiors begin with beautiful spaces. I would rather my clients invest in refining the background and build up their furnishings slowly over time, than attempt to hide a poorly executed space behind distracting fabrics and furnishings.

The truth is that every project presents an opportunity for me to use my creative powers and envision the possibilities long before I share my first thoughts with my clients and my staff. Those first moments spent in a new space quietly observing are, for me, some of the most enjoyable times spent. They are moments that I use to take in a space, fresh and unencumbered by outside opinions and discussions of budgets and time schedules. It is an exciting exercise in pure design analysis, a time to simply react to and discover the strengths and weaknesses of a space. All of

this is taking place in my head, a private and creative stream of consciousness that plays like a video that only I can see.

For the viewer who enters into a wonderful interior, it is that sensation that everything around them feels right. It can be an almost unconscious recognition that the room had no other solution than to be as it is. I do not believe you need to be a professional in the world of design to figure this out. I am also certain that we all can sense when something feels *wrong*. This is all related to that human connection we make to spaces. Finding the solutions is another story. It is something that requires thought, experience, and understanding of what is *wrong* and what is *right* in order to plot the direction of what a space can be become.

In the following pages, you will see photos that expose some of the real challenges of my first moments experiencing spaces that are far from perfect. These images represent some of the realities that we are all confronted with as we attempt to create our "perfect" environments. The before and after images are presented to help you better understand my process and give deeper insight into the thought and planning that go on long before the furnishings, art, and collections are placed.

UPDATING TRADITION

When looking at existing spaces, I try to find ways to build up the background. Expanding a space, even slightly, can allow you to increase the scale of the architectural features, leading you to a space that remains traditional while projecting a modern confidence. This Virginia dining room once suffered from modest details and limited light. By expanding the space only four feet, I was able to substantially increase the architectural impact and strengthen its connection to the past.

SIMPLY ILLUMINATING

Some spaces take more than one glance to appreciate what they may have to offer. My first impression of this apartment was that it felt dark and claustrophobic. The first step was to open it up to natural light and then strip away all of the unnecessary architectural features. I wanted to start over and bring in subtle new details that would create a sense of light and air. These simple gestures helped me bring new energy and a modern ease to the apartment.

Before

After

307

REFINED FOCUS WITH A LIGHT TOUCH

Some spaces only require slight architectural refinements to transform them. This library offered me a good vocabulary, but the room lacked focus. Installing a bold fireplace elevation helped me bring strength to the room. I used soft midtone fabrics to blend with the color of the existing pine paneling. bringing a seamless unity between the architecture and the furnishings. This harmony allows the eye to roam easily throughout the space rather than being distracted by startling blocks of upholstery.

MOVE ON

Knowing when a space needs to be totally redesigned is a valuable asset. Too much time and money are spent trying to revive bad ideas from the past. No successful room can be built around a bad foundation. Here in this breakfast room, I was confronted with a low ceiling, dark brick, and no easy fix. The old raised fireplace made the low ceiling appear lower than it actually was. I began by designing a new system of brightly painted paneling that would softly bring interest to the walls and remove the weight of the imposing brick wall. The result is a room that is perfectly balanced.

Before

After

THE BLANK SLATE

Often projects only offer you open space with no existing architectural vocabulary to build on. This raw apartment on Central Park South was an endless string of windows that looked out on amazing park views. Determining the architectural style of this space was the first step in developing its interior. A layering of contrasting wall surfaces added depth and dimension to the simplicity of the floor plan.

ROMANCE REBORN

Some rooms may contain perfect proportions that are hidden behind bad detailing or insensitive remodeling. Over time, the many renovations of this home in Southampton had diluted its original charm. The garden outside inspired my use of white plaster treillage to bring a quiet elegance back to this dining room. The goal here was to rebuild the space in a way that would reflect the spirit of the house, not the date of my renovation.

Before

After

"Inspiration is not replication. It is taking an experience and allowing it to filter through your own sensibilities so when it comes out, it comes out new."

– Thomas Pheasant

Acknowledgments

With Appreciation

I consider myself fortunate to have received so much from the brilliant designers and architects, both past and present, who have created amazing works that inspire and propel me to be better.

I dedicate this book to my family and friends, whose belief in me means everything, to every client who trusts me to guide them, and every employee who over the past many years has worked under my roof in efforts to support my vision.

I am most appreciative that after thirty years, I still have the desire and passion to continue on my own path of design, knowing that perfection is not a destination but merely a motivation. Every new project brings a new opportunity to move forward in finding my voice.

To those who read this book, it is my sincere hope that my thoughts and images contribute something to your journey and understanding that there is a power within the walls of a serene interior that can change us and provide us room to dream, create, and evolve.

Thomas Pheasant

Inspirational Photography

Interior Photography

Durston Saylor
I, 12 *lower left / lower right*, 17, 25, 27, 28, 34, 35, 39, 47, 48, 54, 55, 57, 62, 63, 65 *left / right*, 66, 67, 69, 80, 83, 87, 89, 94, 95, 97, 100, 103, 114, 117, 126, 128 *left*, 129, 134, 143, 145, 147, 148, 149 *left*, 156, 159, 161, 163 *lower right*, 164 *upper right*, 165, 166, 167 *upper center / lower center*, 168 *upper right / center left*, 172, 173, 177, 179, 180, 181, 182, 185, 186, 187, 188, 201, 206, 208, 209, 211, 213, 214, 215, 216 *left / right*, 217, 219, 220, 221, 223 *upper right / lower left*, 224, 225, 227, 256, 257, 259, 261, 265, 266, 267, 268, 269, 270, 271, 276, 277, 279, 281 *lower left*, 282, 283, 290, 291, 293, 294, 295, 304, 308, 310, 312, 314

Saylor / *Architectural Digest*; © Condé Nast
21, 23, 24, 29, 40, 107, 157, 288

Thomas Pheasant
6, 12 *upper left / upper center / upper right / center left / center / center right / lower center*, 74, 115, 116, 123, 124, 150, 163 *upper left / upper right / center right*, 164 *center left / lower center*, 167 *upper left / upper right / center left / center / center right / lower left / lower right*, 168 *upper left / lower left / lower center / lower right*, 200, 223 *upper left / lower right*, 234, 236, 237, 239, 241 *upper / lower*, 242, 243, 244, 247 *upper center / upper right / center right / lower left / lower right*, 248 *upper left / center right / lower left / lower center / lower right*, 249, 250, 263 *all*, 281 *upper right*, End Pages

Gordon Beall
X, 10, 16, 19, 20, 37, 41, 43, 44, 45, 49, 75, 77, 79, 84, 85, 86, 98, 101, 102, 105, 106, 108, 119, 120, 121, 125 *left / right*, 127, 128 *right*, 135, 139, 140, 149 *right*, 151, 162, 163 *upper center / lower left*, 164 *upper left / lower left / lower right*, 175, 183, 184, 197, 281 *upper left / lower right*, 285, 286, 317

Beall / *Architectural Digest*; © Condé Nast
109, 122, 287

Max Kim-Bee
IV, XII, 59, 81, 144, 306

Chris Leaman
3

Xavier Béjot
front cover, 137, 138, 232, 233, 245, 247 *upper left*, 248 *upper right*, 251

Walter Smalling
142, 178

Diana Parrish Design and Photography
194, 196

Ping Amranand
189

Architecture

Shope Reno Wharton Architects
27, 28, 55, 67, 83, 103, 173

David Jones Architects
10, 109, 122, 135

Rill & Decker Architects
39

Hartman-Cox Architects
40

ISBN-13: 978-0-8478-4081-6
Library of Congress Control Number: 2013933279

2020 / 10 9 8 7
Distributed to the U.S. Trade by Random House, New York
Printed and bound in China

Photography credits appear on pages 321–322.
Graphic Design by Streetsense

300 Park Avenue South,
New York, NY 10010

www.rizzoliusa.com